NEA
EARLY CHILDHOOD
ED

D0861712

Problem Solving in the Early Childhood Classroom

Joan Britz
Norma Richard

A NATIONAL EDUCATION ASSOCIATION
P U B L I C A T I O N

Copyright © 1992
National Education Association of the United States

Printing History
  First Printing: January 1992

Note

The opinions expressed in this publication should not be construed as representing the policy or position of the National Education Association. Materials published by the NEA Professional Library are intended to be discussion documents for educators who are concerned with specialized interests of the profession.

Library of Congress Cataloging-in-Publication Data

Britz, Joan.
    Problem solving in the early childhood classroom / Joan Britz,
    Norma Richard.
            p. cm. —(NEA Early childhood education series)
        Includes bibliographical references.
        ISBN 0-8106-0360-8
        1. Early childhood education—United States. 2. Problem solving.
    I. Richard, Norma. II. Title. III. Series: Early childhood
    education series (Washington, D.C.)
    LB1139.25.B76 1992
    372.21—dc20   91–21688
                                         CIP

CONTENTS

For C., who taught me that dreams do come true.

J. B.

To Diann Hoffman for her friendship and for helping me to see many possibilities

And to Walter, Jesse, and Jonathan for their patience, support, and endless understanding.

N. R.

Acknowledgments

With grateful thanks to my teacher, Dr. Ida Santos Stewart; mentors Paula Jorde Bloom and Marilyn Sheerer; computer experts Steve, Doug, and Joe; exceptional early childhood teachers Kathy Koeppel, Rita DiVito, Erik Hansen, Linda Smitty, and Nancy Buttino; and editor Nance Schuster for their trust, encouragement, confidence, and support.

J. B.

I am grateful for the support and friendship of my colleagues at Baker Demonstration School, National-Louis University. I am especially indebted to Ann Watson, whose insightful problem-solving experience with her first graders appears in Chapter 2, and to Beth Kolehmainen and Terrie Bridgman for their suggestions, ideas, support, and good spirits.

I wish to express special thanks to Marilyn Sheerer. Without her cheerful encouragement this work would never have been accomplished.

N. R.

The Authors

Joan Britz is Faculty Coordinator of Early Childhood Education Undergraduate Certification at National-Louis University, Chicago.

Norma Richard is a Kindergarten Teacher at the Baker Demonstration School, National-Louis University, Evanston campus.

The Advisory Panel

Noreen L. Barney, Third Grade Teacher, Huckleberry Hill School, Brookfield, Connecticut; and Geography Consultant for Connecticut Geographic Alliance

Adele Bergen, Adjunct Professor, Humanities Division, Bergen Community College, Paramus, New Jersey

Patricia H. Bleazey, Kindergarten Teacher, Lanier Elementary School, Maryville, Tennessee

J. Colleen Bross, Kindergarten Teacher, Grandview Elementary School, Higginsville, Missouri

Constance Fay, Nursery Teacher, Hintil Kuu Ca Child Development Center, Oakland Public Schools, California; Oakland Education Association Board Member, Liaison for Child Development Center Teachers; member of NEA Early Childhood Caucus

Arlene Hett, Assistant Professor of Early Childhood Education, College of Great Falls, Montana

Martha Mitchell, Parent Infant Coordinator, Zanesville City Schools, Ohio

Carolyn Webber, Kindergarten Teacher, Belvedere Elementary School, Anne Arundel County, Maryland

OVERVIEW: USING THIS BOOK

This book has been carefully designed so you can gain the most information in the least amount of time. We know from our own experience that time is critical to the teachers of young children.

Chapter 1 introduces problem solving and presents various viewpoints to be considered as you become familiar with the topic. Some of this information you may already know; some of this information may be new to you.

Chapter 2 is a practical presentation of constructivism, the work of Piaget, and how problem solving relates to learning. Examples make this an easy-to-read and easy-to-understand explanation of the theory used as the foundation of our writings. It is important that the reader understand the basic philosophy behind using problem solving in early childhood classrooms.

Chapter 3 includes many strategies and techniques for using problem solving with individuals and with groups. Its examples are woven into the fabric of the last chapters.

Chapters 4 through 8 are arranged for teachers of children aged 4 through 8. (Chapter 4 is for teachers of four-year-olds, and Chapter 6 is for teachers of first graders.) We are aware that multiage classrooms are the most appropriate ways to group young children, but we also know that teachers are often hired as "the kindergarten teacher" or "the first grade teacher." Because arranging the chapters for your easy reference was a priority, we chose to include a chapter for each grade level. It is our hope that you will begin with the chapter that most applies to the children in your classroom, but also read the other chapters. Each one contains information, ideas, examples, and strategies that may be just what you are searching for. We hope that you will find time to read all the chapters. We hope that this book will solve all your problems about problem solving.

Chapter 1

PROBLEM SOLVING AND YOUNG CHILDREN

The kindergarten room is a busy place. Groups of children are scattered around the room, talking as they work and using manipulatives. Some are acting out a drama with costumes they have made themselves, some are writing a book together, some are sorting objects, and the children at one table are working on cards for a classmate. Two children are "fishing" side by side at similar magnetic games.

"Let's put all the pieces from both games together into one tub," says Shauna. "Then we can separate all the numbers from the letters. It will be fun," she says as she moves closer to Raul.

"Wait. Wait. My hooker [the magnet at the end of the fishing pole] is sticking to yours. What can we do?" asks Raul.

Shauna continues to wiggle her line closer to Raul's line. "Look at this. I can make my pole catch yours," says Shauna as the magnets meet. "Let's see if we can use the poles to catch some letters."

They try coordinating the pulling movements on each of their poles and do indeed "catch" three letters from the pond. "That was neat. Now let's separate the lines," says Raul.

The children move apart, but the magnets still stick together.

"How can we get these apart?" Shauna reaches toward the magnets, but Raul pulls his pole away. "Don't touch," says Raul. The new rule is that you can't touch with your hands. Let's find a new way to get them apart. Let's figure out this problem.

This is problem solving.

Problem solving has always been a part of the learning of the young child. Observe a baby use a variety of solutions to reach a toy behind a chair. Watch a toddler figure out how to get up onto a rocking chair. A preschooler cries until he is given the toy he wants. A kindergartner cleverly negotiates with playmates until she can take her turn first. Observe a primary-age child learning to break a reading code. These are examples of problem solving at work both in the child's ordinary life and in the classroom setting.

DEFINING PROBLEM SOLVING

Years ago, the topic of problem solving was rarely included in books relating to learning and young children. Occasionally chapters on science or mathematics would suggest problem solving as a goal, but little else was included to help the teacher plan and facilitate this part of the curriculum.

Problem solving differs from academic learning. It supports curiosity and discovery because it is immediate, observable, and obvious. The process of problem solving encourages autonomous thinking in children and thrives in a cooperative learning environment. Deductive reasoning, as well as trial and error, is inherent in the problem-solving process. Knowledge and learning gained through problem solving can be used in new and meaningful ways. Diligent teachers must search for strategies to promote problem solving in all areas of the curriculum.

Traditionally, problem solving has been included only in the mathematics and science sections of the curriculum. Yet problem solving should be an integral part of every facet of the curriculum from early literacy, including writing, reading, listening, and speaking, to social studies, music, art, and movement. Problem solving provides an integrated way for the young child to learn and meets the needs of the whole child—emotional, social, cognitive, and physical. An integrated teaching plan is the best way to reflect how children really learn and to help them discover problem solving for themselves.

Problem solving is a dynamic learning process for young children. It is decisionmaking through spontaneous investigation, exploration, and experimentation. It means pursuing understanding, looking for answers, trying out some possibilities, and finding out whether or not they work. Problem solving helps children become aware of alternatives, cope with difficulty, and feel empowered, rather than vulnerable.

Whether the source of the problem to be investigated is the teacher or the child's spontaneous interest, the problem-solving experience must occur in a context that is meaningful to the child. The focus is on the child and the active process of solving a problem, rather than on finding an answer. Active problem solving is the means by which young children are motivated to extend their thinking and build mental relationships.

WHY USE PROBLEM SOLVING?

Young children eagerly pursue problems to solve even without adult intervention. Given the opportunity, young children seem compelled to actively explore their environment. In an experimental parent-toddler class made up of children 16 months to 2 years of age, teachers noticed that even these very young children began to organize their toys by size, color, and shape without any adult to tell them that these things were important. One child lined up little cars in a long row, more or less by size. Another toddler began to place plastic shapes side by side according to color. Another child spent 20 minutes stacking her materials by shape.

From this experience, preprimary and primary teachers began to question not only how they taught, but also why they taught certain things to older children. It was astonishing for these teachers to realize that if very young children have already thought about such concepts as color, shape, and size, why do teachers focus on teaching preschool and kindergarten children these same concepts that they have known since they were 16 months old? Teachers went on to speculate about how the role of the teacher as the central communicator of information would have to change. They asked, "If children teach themselves, what does the teacher do?"

This book on problem solving is an attempt to answer these vital questions. It is also intended to be a beginning for teachers who wish to incorporate a more child-centered approach into their teaching. As teachers, we sometimes forget the value of supporting problem-solving strategies for children. We focus on giving answers, rather than on encouraging children to validate their own experiences and ideas (Duckworth 1987; Kamii & DeVries 1973, 1980).

Teachers can respond in two ways to children's enthusiasm concerning their own personal investigation. Teachers might encourage children to explore and think further about what is meaningful to them, or they might insist that children learn what the *adult* thinks they should learn from the experience. The former choice opens up myriad possibilities for children to develop self-esteem, mastery, and knowledge of their world. The latter choice closes opportunities for children to make understanding personally meaningful.

The ability to generate solutions to problems promotes a sense of competence for children. The "I did it!" response encourages children to rely on their own abilities, rather than on an adult, to decide how to accomplish a task. The adult never abdicates the central position of facilitator and organizer for children. Yet the teacher who values children's autonomy and strategies for problem solving as a foundation for curriculum understands that it is through self-regulated play, activity, and investigation that preprimary and primary children are free to build a meaningful understanding of reality (Forman & Kuschner 1983).

THE CHALLENGE OF PROBLEM SOLVING

What, then, is so new and exciting about problem solving for young children in the nineties? Instead of an auxiliary skill that is tacked onto lesson plans and introduced at the close of lessons, problem solving has evolved into a critical skill of primary importance in the early childhood curriculum. Problem solving has become the focus of the education of young children. This importance of problem solving as the focal point in the curriculum is what is new and exciting.

What has initiated this new emphasis? A consensus of viewpoints, an examination of the meaning of knowledge, the strengthening of professional education organizations and of the National Association for the Education of Young Children (NAEYC), and the future direction of American society are all elements that have served to increase the emphasis on problem solving in the early childhood curriculum.

A CONSENSUS OF VIEWPOINTS

Developmentally Appropriate Practice (Bredekamp), a 1987 NAEYC publication, outlines the important components of the education of young children. This extensive guide for the best education and care of children from birth to 8 years of age is supported by the vast majority of early childhood educators from all types of programs—Head Start, Montessori, private, and public schools. It represents the first accumulation of ideas agreed on by the early childhood community. Following are three important guidelines included in this book.

1. The curriculum should be integrated, with skills and knowledge overlapping, because this is the way young children learn.
2. Problem solving, choices, and decision making are integral parts of the curriculum.
3. The role of the teacher is to facilitate learning by

preparing the environment, to provide materials that are appropriate for each individual, and to extend and expand learning as it occurs.

With the publication and wide distribution of this NAEYC publication on developmentally appropriate practice, early childhood educators, for the first time, have a concise and extensive guide to follow that outlines classroom practices and curriculum. This publication has given new emphasis and importance to problem solving for young children.

DEFINING KNOWLEDGE IN EARLY CHILDHOOD

John Dewey

The work of John Dewey demonstrates the function of problem solving in the child-centered curriculum for the young child. According to Dewey (1966), the curriculum should be built on the interests of the individual child. Problem solving, inquiry, and discovery facilitate cognitive growth. Social growth, especially necessary for a democratic society, is promoted by problem-solving interactions with others in the group. Dewey writes:

The accumulation and acquisition of information for purposes of reproduction in recitation and examination is made too much of. "Knowledge," in the sense of information, means the working capital, the indispensable resources of further inquiry, of finding out, or learning, more things.Frequently, it is treated as an end in itself, and then the goal becomes to heap it up and display it when called for. This static, cold-storage ideal of knowledge is inimical to educative development. It not only lets occasions for thinking go unused, but it swamps thinking. No one could construct a house on ground cluttered with miscellaneous junk. Pupils who have stored their "minds" with all kinds of material which they have never put to intellectual uses are sure to be hampered when they try to think. They have no practice in selecting what is appropriate. (1966, p. 158)

The "indispensable resources of further inquiry, of finding out, or learning, more things" comprise problem solving. Problem solving must be the foundation of education for the young child.

Jean Piaget

The work of Jean Piaget is useful to educators because it enables them to better understand how children think and learn. Piaget's work represents a means by which teachers gain insights into the nature of children's thinking and the stages of their intellectual development. It is valuable for teachers to understand why it is difficult for four-year-olds to tell time, to understand the adult concept of fairness, or to say "My fish died because it was in the water too long." It is helpful for second or third grade teachers to understand that even third graders' thinking may still be characterized by egocentric and magical elements.

Another valuable contribution of Piaget's work for early childhood teachers lies in the understanding that, for children eight years old and younger, thinking is still closely related to physical action. For Piaget, children's physical actions on materials is inextricably tied to their mental actions. The kinds of problem-solving activities that promote mental development during the early childhood years are those that fascinate children, those that allow children to control their own efforts, and those that are play-oriented and genuinely experimental in nature (DeVries & Kohlberg 1987).

DeVries and Kohlberg contend that schools create many learning disabilities through their failure to adapt teaching to the way children think and through their insistence that children learn what they cannot yet understand. A problem solving approach would help to correct this problem because it fosters a curriculum that is sensitive to individual developmental needs. Piaget teaches that intellegence is best developed through the kinds of experiences in which children actively solve problems that are important to them. This happens when children are faced with explaining phenomena or when they have individual goals to pursue (Piaget & Garcia 1971, as found in DeVries & Kohlberg 1987). Piaget describes the reason why teachers should support children's active and spontaneous investigation:

> Only this [spontaneous] activity, oriented and constantly stimulated by the teacher, but remaining free in its attempts, its tentative efforts, and even its errors, can lead to intellectual independence. It is not by knowing the Pythagorean theorem that free exercise of personal reasoning power is assured; it is in having rediscovered its existence and usage. The goal of intellectual education is not to know how to repeat or retain ready-made truths (a truth that is parroted is only a half truth). It is in learning to master the truth by oneself at the risk of losing a lot of time and of going through all the roundabout ways that are inherent in real activity. (1948, pp. 105–106)

In this passage, Piaget elaborates on the notion that children's spontaneous problem-solving activity is of great importance for their intellectual development. Piaget also emphasizes that it is the teacher who facilitates this process by creating a stimulating environment and by allowing children the freedom to accomplish their goals in their own way.

PROFESSIONAL ORGANIZATIONS

The collective voice of Americans committed to the education and well-being of young children has become stronger over the past few years as the membership of professional associations continues to grow. Through its bimonthly magazine, *Young Children*, the NAEYC is a voice raising professional concerns, advocating on behalf of young children, and calling for use of the most current classroom practices within the field of early childhood education. NAEYC supporters are convinced that by providing a curriculum rich in problem solving, choices, and decisionmaking, quality education will be assured for young children in schools across the United States. The National Education Association (NEA) also promotes quality schools and, through a series of media announcements, has informed the American taxpayer of its thoughts on new directions for American education.

THE AMERICAN SOCIETY OF THE FUTURE

Megatrends 2000 (Naisbitt & Aburdene 1990), a collection of facts and predictions relating to the future, identifies new directions for the 1990s. Two of these directions specifically relate to the education of young children.

First, Naisbitt and Aburdene discuss the globalism anticipated in the future. "The world is becoming more and more cosmopolitan, and we are all influencing each other," states designer Paloma Picasso (p. 22). Multicultural education and problem solving go hand in hand. To survive in the new American society, children must be able to hold onto their values and yet be flexible to adapt to the new traditions and cultures of which they are becoming a part. The process of problem solving encourages the learner to look for diversity in solutions. This diversity may very well begin with the ethnic, religious, and cultural heritage of families in the United States. Problem solving is enriched by becoming aware of a variety of viewpoints and by negotiating to reach a common solution.

Second, the "triumph of the individual" in the future certainly implies the need for problem-solving skills. According to the authors, the individual will become competent not by acquiring knowledge by rote, but rather by learning to solve problems creatively, including those yet to be identified. The skills and techniques needed to meet this challenge must be introduced early, practiced often, and expanded throughout the school years.

These two directions of the future, as identified in *Megatrends 2000*, speak again to the need for basing education on problem solving. Our educational system cannot turn its back on the children of the future. We must give these children the skills they need to succeed in the years ahead.

Chapter 2

HOW CHILDREN LEARN

Teachers who support children's problem-solving strategies in the classroom do so because they are convinced that children somehow learn "better" this way. Do children learn better? Why is problem solving a value for early childhood professionals? The work of Jean Piaget can help us understand why problem-solving strategies complement an active, integrated, child-centered teaching approach.

CHILDREN CONSTRUCT KNOWLEDGE

Piaget's constructivist theory demonstrates that knowledge evolves for all of us through the internal process of inventing understanding for ourselves. Simply put, we build knowledge from inside our minds, rather than from the outside in. Kamii and DeVries (1973, 1980) describe constructivism as "the process by which an individual evolves his own adaptive intelligence and knowledge" (p. 372). The notion that children must construct knowledge for themselves, rather than having the teacher "instruct" them, radically changes the way we teach, how we deal with children in the classroom, and our understanding of how children learn.

WHAT IS LEARNING FOR YOUNG CHILDREN?

Constructivism teaches us that children learn best by actively involving themselves, in a physical way, in their environment. Young children actually think better when they are free to act on the objects and materials around them (Williams & Kamii 1986). When teachers support investigating, inspecting, manipulating materials, building, comparing, questioning, and

20

exploring among preprimary and primary children, they allow these children to actively use their intelligence.

Knowledge From the Physical World

Children learn about the world in two different ways: through knowledge that is partly external to them and through knowledge that is internal to them. External or physical knowledge is the kind of understanding that can be observed in the physical world. Children touch, feel, pull, and manipulate objects and, in general, physically act on their environment in order to learn about reality. By bouncing a ball, balancing blocks, feeling the weight of clay, and noticing the color of leaves, children can observe and experience physical properties. Because of Piaget's work, we know now that young children should not be passively using worksheets or memorizing facts or learning from pictures, rather than experience. Instead, they should be actively investigating the objects around them and finding out what kinds of reactions will result (Kamii & DeVries 1980).

Knowledge Through Mental Activity

A second way that children learn is internal to each individual. Children understand not through observation and action alone, but also through their own mental activity. Piaget calls this mental action logico-mathematical knowledge. This knowledge is created when children construct relationships between and among objects that cannot be seen in external reality.

A first grader, for example, makes a chart comparing his eye color with other children in the class. A 4-year-old examines the difference between two dots and three dots in a game with dice. Third graders compare the similarities between two kinds of invertebrates, worms and bees. Mental relationships, such as *same, different, similar, number,* and *comparisons,* must be created in the mind of the individual and cannot be seen in physical reality. The child sees the dice or the eye colors, but the relationship of the sameness or the difference in dice or eye colors is constructed by the child in her mind. Piaget contends that logico–mathematical knowledge cannot be taught and must be invented by the child. Therefore, it is the connection between the mental and the physical actions that is important and that enables the child to understand more.

FACILITATING LEARNING

Encouraging Problem Solving

If children cannot be taught and must invent mental relationships for themselves, what can teachers do to help young children learn? Williams and Kamii (1986) describe three ways to encourage children to invent their own ways to solve problems.

Activities Must Be Personally Meaningful

The first strategy is to connect classroom activities with what is personally meaningful to children. The natural life of the classroom is a good way to encourage meaningful problem-solving activities. Negotiating alternative ways for deciding who goes first in a board game, asking four-year-olds to set the table and put one cup for each chair, and voting to decide what playground to visit are examples of spontaneous ways children can think more about their environment.

Another example happened in a kindergarten classroom when children were complaining about a schoolwide lottery that was conducted to raise money for disadvantaged children. The children were upset that the winning ticket was a number that no one had bought. In effect, they felt no one had won. Five children decided to write a letter to the student council asking that another number be drawn so that someone could win. They drew pictures representing disappointed children with their lottery tickets. They dictated the letter to the teacher and signed their names.

They also decided that if their request was denied, they could conduct their own classroom lottery. Several children made blank tickets, others drew money in various denominations, and still others made "baskets" to hold the tickets. Some children went to each individual child, explained the game, and had them write a number, their name, and the teacher's name on the ticket. Decisions had to be made, such as how each child would know what number was his, what kind of prizes would be given, and whether there should be more than one winner. What did the children learn from this experience? They learned to solve problems concerning literacy, mathematics, and science (how to construct a basket out of paper) and how to solve social and emotional conflicts. A great deal of the motivation for this project resulted from the fact that it was personally meaningful to the children.

Encourage Decision-Making Strategies

A second way to encourage thinking is to provide opportunities for children to make decisions. When a teacher makes all the decisions about classroom affairs, then the children cannot invent ways to solve problems. If the teacher wants a weather chart for the children to use in the classroom, the children learn more if they make it. They can decide in a small group if the rules of "no peeking" in a card game should be changed. They also can decide as a group what stategies to use when no one wants to cleanup after free activity time. Older children can make decisions about alternative ways to solve mathematics problems or how to deal with the problem of students treating substitute teachers badly.

Encourage Peer Interaction

A third way Williams and Kamii describe for supporting thinking with young children is to encourage them to work together to solve problems. By providing opportunities for children to exchange viewpoints, the teacher allows an exchange in which children actually think harder about what they are doing. Johnson and Johnson's (Johnson, Johnson et al. 1984) cooperative learning strategies for primary children encourage them to talk about issues that each child may see quite differently. When children argue their points of view and negotiate with peers, then the possibility for thinking more broadly is maximized. When the teacher controls all the answers by making decisions for the children and by insisting that they work individually, rather than collaboratively, then the possibility of problem solving is diminished.

Rote Learning Inhibits Problem Solving

Unfortunately, many early childhood teachers are unable to emphasize problem solving because they focus on rote learning and the teaching of specific information. They believe that children learn by passively looking at pictures, memorizing many different facts, filling out worksheets, and performing teacher–oriented skills. Teachers who focus on these things may never stop to consider whether young children can connect this information with their own experience. Teachers need to ask themselves how meaningful the things they teach children are from the children's point of view. When teachers teach material by telling the children what or how to think, then these children cannot invent it for themselves, nor can they initiate the process of understanding. Additionally, the children's self-esteem suffers.

Planting seeds can be an activity in which the teacher tells the children what to think, or it can be an activity in which the teacher helps the children to think about the experience at their own level. For example, a teacher can tell younger children to count the seeds, print the names of the seeds, or memorize the various kinds of seeds on a tray. The children learn specific information like "This is a tomato seed." Older children might memorize the growth pattern of seeds or learn to recite the different parts of a plant. These are examples of specific, rote kinds of learning.

This same activity can help children to think more broadly. Children might learn to classify a variety of objects as "plantable" or not, or as "growable" or not. Older children can investigate why you cannot grow a tree from an apple seed, or they might conduct soil and plant experiments. Even very young children can process this activity at their own level. For example, one preprimary teacher used the following problem-solving activity with her three- and four-year-olds. She put out a tray with a variety of seeds, fruit pits, and small rocks. Before planting, she asked the children what would happen if they planted everything on the tray. What would grow? After a lively discussion and much thought, some children felt that the seeds would grow, but that the rocks would not "because rocks are not flowers." Others thought that if some seeds did not grow, you should "plant them upside down." Others said that rocks will grow with special care, like "pinch the rock three times" and then plant it and "water it a lot!" In this activity, children thought a great deal about planting, and they exchanged viewpoints about what they thought.

What Children's Mistaken Ideas Tell Us

Younger children tend to reveal how differently they think about the world. Through language and behavior, they show the process by which they assimilate specific information into what they already know. One kindergarten teacher described a five-year-old in her class who said, "Teacher, I could tell time if I could only get the hands on the clock to stop moving!" Though amusing to adults, these creative ideas are children's attempts to classify, organize, and build coherence from what they already know to what they do not know. Specific information has meaning for children only in the context of the broad sense of knowledge. DeVries and Kohlberg (1987) state that a child's erroneous ideas reflect her or his unique and subjective experiences. Children begin to refine "incorrect" answers as they broaden their understanding. Learning then is not merely a passive accumulation of knowledge; it is also the active ability to use intelligence. Problem solving, rather than rote learning alone, builds broader knowledge and helps children make sense of their world.

Problem Solving as an Active Process

Current child development research teaches that children learn in a holistic way and that learning is a dynamic, active process for children. It is a process in which understanding is created through the simultaneous interaction of physical, social, emotional, and intellectual experiences. Constructivism demonstrates that thinking is the integrating factor in development. Problem solving, then, is an experience that must address the whole thinking, feeling, physical child.

What kinds of problem-solving experiences are best for children? Teachers must allow opportunities for children to actively investigate the causes and effects of their actions and thoughts on their environment. The aim is to support children's decision-making ability, to free them from dependence on the teacher for answers, and to help them evaluate what they believe to be valid.

Help Children Explore Possibilities

Freeing children to think for themselves is a difficult task in itself. Our system of education, with its emphasis on "right" answers, typically inhibits children from exploring possibilities. Even very young children are already aware that teachers control the correct way to think about things. A good way to break down this kind of dependence is to encourage children to express a variety of viewpoints. Reflecting everyone's perspective in a nonjudgmental way not only lets children know that their opinion is respected, but also allows them to move toward autonomy. Voting, giving children choices about activities, engaging in cooperative learning in small groups, encouraging questions, and allowing mistakes tell children that their investigation is valued.

Encourage Strategies for Finding Solutions

The ability to create solutions to problems also promotes a sense of competence for children. The best kinds of problems for children to solve are not necessarily always academic. Social or emotional conflicts provide good problems for children to investigate and solve. "We decided to take turns using this game" and "I'm going to use the game later so she will have time to play with it now" are examples of how problem solving is used in all areas of development.

The teacher remains firmly in charge, but offers ways for the children to think about the problem. "We have a problem here. You both want to use the same game. What can we do about it?" Two children who want the same material can fight over it or see it as a problem to be solved. The teacher can begin by helping the children perceive the problem as separate from themselves. When children are able to view the consequences of their actions, then they begin to develop a sense of mastery. "Good" problems are those that both are meaningful for children and present a challenge (Galinsky 1989).

Encouraging children to become aware of all the problem-solving possibilities enables them to actively investigate the causes and effects of their actions and thoughts on their environment. They learn decision making, how to ask questions, and how to evaluate what they think is true. In short, they learn the complex process of thinking for themselves. It is active learning at its best.

THE TEACHER'S ROLE IN PROBLEM SOLVING

The teacher has a central role in supporting problem-solving efforts because it is the teacher who facilitates the process for the children. The early childhood teacher is child-centered, creates an integrated curriculum, and strives to build reciprocal relationships with the children. In addition, the teacher makes use of the following strategies to connect the children with problem-solving opportunities.

1. Create an environment that supports the children's autonomy.
2. Choose problems that the children can actively investigate.
3. Offer activities that enable the children to solve problems in a meaningful context.
4. Use language that opens up possibilities for problem solving.

The Problem-Solving Environment

The classroom environment is created by the teacher, and the quality of that environment is critical in determining how free the children will be to learn. If teachers are to be effective in their efforts to stimulate the children's interest in meaningful problems, they must pay attention not only to the kinds of activities they present, but, more importantly, to how they approach and interact with the children engaged in problem-solving activities. Through classroom relationships, teachers give permission for the children to take the initiative in solving problems, to offer personal opinions, and to find that being mistaken is allowed.

Many teachers face the problem of convincing children that their opinions are valued. Often children are reluctant to offer suggestions because they may be contrary to what the teacher wants or may not be correct. Early in the year, one second grade teacher asked her class to give opinions concerning classroom rules. It took her quite a while to help the children understand that she wanted their real views. But at the next opportunity, the teacher found that the children were much less reluctant to express their opinions. The teacher had already succeeded in convincing her students that she valued their autonomy. In a developmentally appropriate classroom, the teacher adapts to the needs of the children, and not the other way around.

Supporting children's autonomy means that the teacher constantly endeavors to understand the children's point of view. The best way for the teacher to understand the children's experience is through observation. Really listening to the children and observing them leads the teacher to understand each child's personal interest and investment in an activity. The teacher can then offer suggestions that help the children extend and elaborate their thinking about a subject and can ask pertinent questions related to the children's goals, rather than imposing predetermined "teacher" goals.

Support Childrens' Active Investigation

Open-ended activities offer daily opportunities for the children to experiment with making decisions, getting immediate feedback, and testing ideas for outcomes. Open-ended activities, as opposed to closed activities are those that can be used in a variety of ways by many children at different levels of understanding. If the children are encouraged to follow their own creative ideas, then they *will* find meaningful problems to solve.

The teacher can begin by putting out a variety of interesting materials and then encourage the children to do as much as they can with them. The children should follow their own interests and ideas, with the teacher structuring only as much of the activity as is necessary to get the children started.

The children can think about mathematics, literacy, art, and other areas of the curriculum in this way. When the teacher notices that the children need help to go further, then a well-placed open-ended question encourages them to reconsider what they are doing and to make the necessary adaptation to test their hypothesis. The children's action is the focus, and not the question or the answer.

The following describes the interactive problem-solving process of Ann, a first grade teacher, who is learning to ask open-ended questions and encourage children to extend their thinking during a mathematics project.

> During activity time, several boys began putting plastic links together in a chain. As it got longer and longer, they became determined to add all the links in the rather large bucket to the chain. It might have ended with them admiring the length of chain and then taking it apart, but it seemed a shame to waste that energetic need to discover something new. My job as teacher was to help them discover even more.
>
> I saw within this project several things that might be learned including counting large numbers, measuring, and counting by tens. But in order for this to be a true discovery experience, the students had to set the problem themselves. *They* had to decide what needed to be learned.
>
> I asked them, "What do you want to find out about the chain?" After thinking, one boy answered, "To see how long it is."
>
> This was a start, but it didn't clearly state the problem in a way that could be worked with. I helped him focus on the problem by clarifying the word *long* with the question, "Do you want to find out how many links long or how many feet long it is?"
>
> First graders aren't always able to express their ideas easily so I gave him the words to use within the question; however, the choice was still his. He and his friends decided they wanted to know how many links they had.
>
> I was concerned about the amount of time needed to do the counting. Here I let my own concerns guide me through the questioning process. A dialogue followed that clarified the problem and the solution.
>
> T: How are you going to find out how many links you have?
> S: We're going to count them.

T: How are you going to count them?

S: By going one, two, three . . . (he pointed to three successive links).

T: (I clarified his procedure) You're going to count by ones?

S: Yea.

The task as they were dealing with it was likely to end in failure when they ran out of time, energy, or knowledge of numbers. But they did not realize this. I commented, "That's a lot of counting. It'll take more time than we have. I wonder if we know another way of counting that will be quicker?"

Students need to be helped to make the connection between the knowledge they possess and the problem to be solved. Our class had been counting by tens all week and was comfortable doing it. One boy made the connection. The final step was working out the procedure for counting by tens. This was done by helping them *see* each new difficulty.

T: I wonder if we know another way of counting that would be quicker?

S: We can count by tens!

T: How will we know when we have ten?

S: We count them.

T: But then we'll be counting by ones again. Can we find a way to put the links together so that we'll be able to just look at them and know we have ten?

S: (No response as students considered the question)

T: I've noticed that you've put many of the same colors together in a row. That's real easy for me to spot. I wonder if there is a way we can use that to help us know when we have ten.

S: (After a thoughtful pause) We could put ten together of the same color.

T: So you'll put ten links together and they'll all be the same color?

S: Uh-huh.

They began connecting the sets of links. At one point, a boy connected two sets of red links. To help him realize and solve the problem, I counted a stretch of links, making sure to count the double set as only ten, rather than the twenty it was. He quickly responded.

S: No that's wrong.

T: I counted by tens.

S: You didn't count all these. (pointing to the second half of the red set)

T: I counted ten for each color I saw. I only saw red.

The boy realized the problem and decided to make sure that each

31

adjoining set in the whole chain was a different color. By the time we were finished, the entire class had put together sets of tens. We finished by counting the links by tens and writing about our problem-solving process.

In summary, I started by asking the boys to define their problem, and then facilitated the process by making observations that brought out potential difficulties, followed by a question that helped them connect known information to this new situation.

This first grade teacher's classroom experience demonstrates thoughtful reflection and practice in asking questions that promote problem solving, autonomy, and self-esteem for her students.

Involve Children in Meaningful Dialogue

Teachers can enhance problem-solving opportunities for children by using language that encourages children to validate their own experience. Rogers, Sheerer Perrin, and Waller (1987) studied teachers' conversations with children. They found that sensitive teachers involve children in meaningful dialogue. These teachers ask questions that encourage open, child-centered conversations, rather than brief, contrived interactions.

Learning to interact with children through sensitive questioning is an important step toward encouraging problem solving. Giving answers to children before they can formulate the problem or consider alternative solutions inhibits the problem-solving process. Likewise, correcting errors in their thinking deters children from making decisions and testing hypotheses. Children refine wrong answers as they think more about something. Teachers must reflect on what children say and do and observe their behavior in order to ask a question that helps the children find solutions.

The example of Ann, the first grade teacher, is a case in point. Ann emphasized her need to ask questions that would enable the children to continue to think about their goal. Her excellent open-ended beginning question—"What do you want to find out about the chain?"—let the children know that their interest and their purpose in the activity were valued by the teacher. Sometimes teachers use language inappropriately. Too many questions distract children from their own ideas. Often a very simple question invites children to think further and to validate the search for a solution.

Solve Problems That Are of Genuine Interest

A major change in the concept of the teacher's role in early childhood education is the move from an adult-centered curriculum to a child-centered one. This means the teacher "instructs" less. It does not at all imply that the teacher abandons the children to do whatever they want in the classroom. Nor does it imply that the curriculum is unplanned. In a child-centered classroom, the teacher is the organizer of materials, space, and activities that provide children with problems to think about. The teacher is also a facilitator, actively intervening in order to help the children work out solutions to problems that are of interest to them. The teacher strives to build an atmosphere of cooperation, collaboration, and mutual respect between herself and the children and among the children themselves (DeVries & Kohlberg 1987).

The role of the teacher is clearly central to the whole process of problem solving for young children. The teacher begins by creating an environment that supports the childrens' autonomy through choices, initiative, and decisionmaking. The teacher then facilitates learning by creating a curriculum that challenges and fascinates the children. The curriculum is enhanced by the teacher's sensitivity to the needs and interests of the children. Thus, the classroom experience is one of mutual respect and reciprocity between teacher and children.

Chapter 3

PROBLEM SOLVING AS PART OF THE CURRICULUM

Problem solving does not just happen. The teacher, as the classroom leader, has the responsibility and the power to *plan, provide,* and *facilitate* problem solving within the educational setting. Here are some ways you can make problem solving happen in your classroom.

PREPARING FOR PROBLEM SOLVING

Changing your classroom from curriculum-centered to child-centered is best brought about, like all change, in small, but important, steps. You may choose to proceed in this way:

1. Write down your observations of the children's problem solving. Think about ways to expand this process. What can you do to enrich these experiences? If you do not observe problem solving occurring, what opportunities have you observed to include problem solving? Why did problem solving not occur? What could you have done to facilitate problem solving?

2. Begin discussing your ideas with another teacher. Duckworth (1987) reminds us that teacher support is important. A co-worker who believes in problem solving can function as a sounding board for your new ideas, infuse additional ideas, and provide evaluative feedback.

3. Think about what you want for your children. What are your teaching goals? What is a curriculum based on problem solving going to do for your children?

Hawkins reminds us that "You don't want to cover a subject; you want to uncover it" (Duckworth, 1987, p. 7). Jot down a few of your goals, and compare them to this list of teacher goals.

- I want each child to become independent.
- I want children to learn firsthand.
- I want children to become excited in learning situations that interest them.
- I want children to take control of their world.
- I want to help each child work better with others.
- I want children to have confidence in their ability to learn.

How do your goals compare with these? Is this what you want for your children? If so, you are ready to change your classroom from a place where the curriculum is important to a place where the child is important.

Learning can occur in either kind of a classroom; it occurs best in a classroom where the child is active, interested, and a true partner in education. By being aware and acknowledging that you want more for your children, you have begun the process of change. For problem solving to become the foundation of an early childhood classroom, you, the teacher, must have confidence that what you are doing is right for young children. Keep your list of goals handy, and refer to them often as the year progresses. This will help you stay on target and include what you want for your children in your everyday planning.

4. Look at your current lesson plans. What would be the best part of the day to begin including problem solving? Let the children take the lead, and focus on

their interests. What would be best for them? What new material or information could you bring to the class that would precipitate new ideas? What group problems are you aware of in your classroom? Plan a time to come together with the children and discuss ways to solve problems. Listen to what they say, and let the children decide solutions. Allow mistakes to happen. We learn from mistakes. Plan time during the day to model problem solving for the children. It is easier to begin problem solving when the children see you doing it.

Problem solving occurs more naturally in some subject areas than in others. These include art, movement, physical education, activities using fluid materials, wood working, cooking, drama, and activities using manipulatives. Because we do not often ask children for wrong or right answers in these subject areas, they are good places in your schedule to begin. Children can often actively try out new ideas in these areas and see the results immediately. Allowing a trial-and-error strategy promotes problem solving. Evaluating results is concrete and immediate. The children can decide for themselves whether the solution works without having to come to you, the teacher.

CHOOSING GOOD PROBLEMS

Goffin and Tull (1985) list the following questions teachers can ask when seeking good problems for young children:

- Is the problem interesting to the child? Is it meaningful?
- Can the child use her knowledge in new situations?
- Must the child make a decision?
- Can the problem be solved at a variety of levels?

- Is the problem easily understood?
- Must concrete actions be taken to gather information? To solve the problem?
- Can the child evaluate these actions?
- Does the problem present opportunities to cooperate and become aware of differing points of view?

Use these questions as guidelines when you are planning for problem solving.

PLANNING FOR PROBLEM SOLVING

It is important to write down lesson plans that include problem solving. Examples of different forms of lesson plans are included in Chapters 4 through 8. Flip through all of these chapters, and find the type of lesson plan that is best for you. Feel free to adapt any of the planning methods that are included. Writing down lesson plans for problem solving will help you focus on what you want to provide, and clarify your ideas, and evaluating your lessons will help you assess the learnings that have occurred. Evaluation will also help you in planning more problem-solving activities for your class and give you the confidence to continue. You will be able to observe the growth that occurs in children and in your curriculum through problem solving.

PROVIDING FOR PROBLEM SOLVING

There are three primary ways in which you can facilitate problem solving: provide time, provide space, and provide materials.

Time

Providing time for problem solving is of critical importance. Duckworth (1987) reminds us that learning occurs with breadth and depth. "If a child spends time exploring all the possibilities of a given notion, it may mean that she holds onto it longer, and moves onto the next stage less quickly; but by the time she does move on, she will have a far better foundation—the idea will serve her far better, will stand up in the face of surprises," states Duckworth (p. 71). This exploration of ideas takes time. A good problem-solving curriculum allows for identifying of ideas, refining those ideas, reaching cooperative solutions, and often rethinking ideas and/or solutions. This probably will not happen all in one lesson, but rather in a series of lessons over a length of time. Duckworth (1987) further states:

> Exploring ideas can only be good, even if it takes time. Wrong ideas, moreover, can only be productive. Any wrong idea that is corrected provides far more depth than if one never had a wrong idea to begin with. You master the idea much more thoroughly if you have considered alternatives, tried to work it out in areas where it didn't work, and figured out why it was that it didn't work, all of which takes time. (p. 71)

Because problem solving is time consuming, an integrated curriculum with subject areas that interconnect and overlap provides the best format for teaching. Large blocks of time and lesson plans with broad goals accommodate necessary learnings. Because standardized testing usually assesses fragmented knowledge, individual facts, and specific skills, problem-solving abilities are often not included. Problem-solving abilities are best assessed through teacher observation. It is the problem-solving process, not the right answer, that is important. Taking the time to observe the problem-solving process is how we best understand the ways children think. When we begin to understand how children think, we can set new challenges and provide new opportunities to expand and extend learnings. By giving children the gift of time, we can encourage them to learn and practice problem-solving skills. We, as teachers, can encourage higher levels of thinking.

Space

If we want problem solving to occur, we must arrange the environment to promote problem solving. Providing space for problem solving often means rearranging desks and tables to facilitate cooperative learning. Physically grouping children together sends them the silent message that it is all right to exchange ideas and to communicate. This exchange of ideas that comes naturally when we arrange the space in this way allows children to hear different viewpoints and encourages them to consider these other points of view. When children are willing to listen and consider other solutions (viewpoints), problem solving becomes a strong mode of learning and negotiation.

When we look at the needs of children, according to Bowers (1990), guidelines for planning the physical environment appear. "Children need to feel safe and secure, gain increasing independence, actively explore a sensory-rich environment, feel competence and self-worth, and interact with a variety of people" (p. 5). Planning space that meets these needs will also promote problem solving. Problem solving can occur in an individual situation, but when groups of learners begin to offer a variety of diverse solutions, the problem-solving experience is enriched. The process of trading ideas and listening to others promotes the social learnings we want for young children.

A special space in your room may be necessary to encourage group work. This can be as grand as an extra table with materials already assembled or as simple as an empty box with paper, pencils, and concrete objects for manipulation. The problem to be solved will formulate the materials needed and also the space. Sometimes groups may need bulletin board space to record and graph ideas, to organize and group pictures, or to provide a display of their ideas. In the role of the resource person for the problem-solving classroom, the teacher provides enough space for the work to be done. Because each classroom is different, the space in each must be allocated differently. It is important for problem solving to have a sense of permanence in the classroom, at least until the group work is completed. By providing enough space for problem solving, the teacher gives an importance and sense of worth to problem-solving projects.

Materials

Including open-ended materials in the learning environment allows children to find a variety of solutions to each problem. Traditionally, preprimary classrooms offer children access to sand, water, brush painting, and woodworking materials. These materials are appropriate for primary-aged children, too. Because children can directly interact and directly control as they manipulate, open-ended materials promote a trial-and-error mode of learning that often is neglected in the first, second, and third grades. Mistakes can be made and answers reworked by the children. For example, when children are provided with a variety of paint colors, brushes in a variety of sizes, and a variety of surfaces on which to paint, problem solving naturally occurs. In contrast, if a child has only one color of paint, one size brush, and one piece of yellow construction paper to use, not many mistakes can be made. The lack of choices prohibits problem solving. Providing a wide diversity of materials that can be used in many different ways encourages exploration where problems can occur. Materials needed for problem solving may include, but should not be limited to, the following:

- Sand and other fluid materials, such as rice, cereal, and and beans
- Water
- Unifix cubes
- Cuisenaire rods
- Counters, especially those from other cultures
- Varieties of papers, paints, brushes, and surfaces
- Woodworking materials and tools
- Blocks of all sizes and shapes

- Measuring cups and spoons
- Tools used to investigate, such as magnifiers, balances, and scales
- Measuring instruments

In classrooms where the space is very limited, these materials can be boxed and labeled so that they can be stored, but are readily accessible to children. Using storage boxes with pictures of the materials shown on the outside of each box is especially important for young children who are nonreaders or who are just beginning to read.

When problem-solving activities begin, ask the children what materials are needed and allow them to help select whatever they need. Package all the materials for a project together to aid in the problem-solving process. Problem solving should not be limited by time, space, or materials.

MODELING A PROBLEM-SOLVING TECHNIQUE

Just as the teacher models being a learner in the early childhood classroom, he can model a four-step method of problem solving in the classroom.

1. Identify the problem.
2. Discuss solutions.
3. Choose a solution and try it out.
4. Evaluate the situation.

Most teachers already are practicing these steps in their classrooms. They often state problems, elicit solution choices, encourage the children to vote on the solution they want to try, and later discuss whether or not the problem is solved. An example of this process might happen like this.

Teacher: Today Julie tripped over a coat on the floor of the coatroom and fell. [Step 1—Identification of the problem] What can we do about this?

Bob: Julie should stay out of the coatroom.

Marie: Everyone should be responsible for hanging up her own coat. Then no one will get hurt.

Juan: We need a coat-closet monitor. Someone should check every day and make sure the coats are all on hooks and not on the floor.

Teacher: Any other ideas? Anything else you want to say?

Mary Jane: I don't think that Julie should have to stay out of the closet because she might need a pencil from her backpack during school. [Step 2—Discussing solutions]

Teacher: Let's vote on the best solution to this problem and see how it helps. Who could help me count hands? [pause as hands are counted] We decided to try all being responsible for our own coats. We'll have to try hard to make sure our coats are always hanging on the hooks. Let's try this for a week and then we can talk about this solution and see if it really solved our problem. [Step 3—Choosing a solution and trying it out]

One week later . . .

Teacher: Last week we voted to each take care of our own coats in the closet and make sure they were hung up. Is this solution to our problem working?

Mark: I think that was a good solution. I'm more careful to make sure my coat is on a hook now.

Julie: There have been no coats on the closet floor this week. We solved our problem. [Step 4—Evaluation]

When the problem-solving process is new to groups of children, the teacher assumes more responsibility and a bigger part in this four-part technique. For instance, the teacher might identify the problem, offer a variety of solutions, ask the children for help in deciding on the best solution, and solicit their evaluative input at the end of the process. As the children become more familiar with using the problem-solving process, the teacher becomes less active in the process and encourages the children to solve problems by themselves. The children would then identify problems, generate solutions, try one solution out, and evaluate the result without any help from the teacher. It is important to allow mistakes to occur—children learn through their own mistakes.

This four-step technique often is not a linear process. Sometimes children identify the wrong problem, and therefore the solutions that are discussed, the one solution that is tried out, and the evaluation may not be appropriate. Sometimes the solutions are not appropriate even if the problem is correctly identified. Often the technique must be used in a circular loop, allowing many different solutions to be tried before the evaluation shows the children that the problem is indeed solved. It is this trial-and-error process that is the very essence of problem solving and is to be encouraged in young children. When children are able to confidently and actively try out ideas, learning occurs.

It is hard for teachers not to step in and assist children as they make mistakes. Teachers want what is best for children. But problem-solving skills can be gained only through practice and only if we, as teachers, allow children to learn in this trial-and-error process.

PROBLEM-SOLVING STRATEGIES

Problems can be solved using a variety of strategies. Some ways children have been observed solving problems include

1. Manipulating actual objects
2. Making a picture of the problem
3. Acting out the problem
4. Talking it over with others
5. Developing a plan
6. Constructing relationships
7. Estimating

Goffin and Tull (1985) remind teachers that to help children become aware of the strategy used, questions such as "How did you know to do that?" and "What did you need to know to solve the problem?" need to be asked (p. 31). By helping children identify the strategies of problem solving, we encourage them to use these strategies more often and more effectively.

The KWL reading strategy, a visual chart format designed by Donna Ogle of National-Louis University for use with children of all ages, helps identify what the participant *knows*, what she *wants* to know, and what she has *learned*. This innovative method of organizing learning experiences combines a variety of problem-solving strategies (making a picture of the problem, talking it over with others, developing a plan, and constructing relationships) and has been used quite effectively to promote group problem solving in the primary grades.

A KWL chart is constructed in the following way. A large piece of paper is divided into three sections, with the headings "What we KNOW" (K), "What we want to WANT to know" (W), and "What we LEARNED" (L). Participants list all they know about the problem (the teacher may need to guide the children as they categorize ideas and facts), write questions that they have about the problem, and, as learning progresses, list all that they have learned. This method of organizing problem solving helps children focus on a variety of solutions before making a final solution choice. It is a systematic way to model the organization of problem solving.

Chapters 4 through 8 will illustrate in detail all of these problem-solving strategies as we look at classrooms at various grade levels. You may wish to read all of these chapters because all problem strategies can be used with children of all ages. The developmental level and the individual interests and needs of the child dictate the problem-solving strategies used in any one instance.

Beginning problem solving with young children is not easy. Traditionally, the teacher's role has been to give correct answers as soon as possible. Waiting and watching as children go through the often slow process of reaching a decision is difficult for a teacher. It may be difficult for the children, too. Here are some opinions expressed by some third graders who recently began classroom activities involving problem solving.

T.A.: Working in groups is hard. You should always have a positive aditude [attitude]. If you're voting for something even if one person kept saying no, don't get mad at them. They're doing what they think is right. Try to understand each other.

K.G.: One idea is to go around to each person and ask if they have ideas and if they do, write them down on paper. Then vote. Then things get done alot faster, believe me, I know.

K.J.: I think working in groups helps people to understand each other more. People learn to communicate better than ushawill [usual]. It helps people who don't like each other become friends.

W.H.: I have learned that when I work in a group you can't have everything that you want. You can work faster in a group. We finished in 3 day(s) and you would probably take 1 whole week.

C.C.: Problem solving ain't no bowl of cherries.

Chapter 4

FOR THE PREKINDERGARTEN TEACHER

PROFILE OF A TEACHER

Kathy is a teacher in a state-funded prekindergarten classroom. She has a background of unusual teaching experiences with young children and families. As a former employee for a state agency providing child and family services and as a foster parent of a special needs child, she brings a rare perspective to her job in the local public school. The experience she gained working with three- and four-year-olds in a private nursery school setting has helped her make the transition of the young children in her public school classroom as easy as possible. Because so much of her teaching life has been spent in community programs, Kathy sees the connection between the school and the community as being critical to the well-being of each family she serves.

I think it is important to always have a housekeeping area available for the children in my program. Children need to work out their roles in the family and to be able to actively make choices. Many times I see separation issues being played out. My job is to observe and try to understand (by what I see and what I hear) just how each child goes about solving problems. This knowledge helps me to enrich and expand the environment for the child. Sometimes I need to ask a question to help a child focus on a problem or to encourage thinking about a problem at a higher level.

Good classrooms for young children must be founded in child development practices. Teachers must not only know child development but must practice it in their own classrooms. When a three-year-old does not want to participate in a group activity, a good teacher reviews her lesson plans to see if the activity was appropriate. She understands that developmentally the behavior of the child was not unusual. The developmental level of the child as well as the individual characteristics of the child should set the pace for all classroom activities.

Children have to figure out what to do with the materials and how to do their own project. Many times I see children who don't know how to begin. They seem afraid of making choices and I have to reassure them that I truly want them to make the choice.

Problem solving helps children develop a sense of autonomy. Children realize that they CAN do it by themselves. This knowledge, in turn, empowers them, builds self-confidence, and promotes creativity. If the teacher provides an environment that has choices, problem solving will happen. Over the years I have grown to trust children more—each child knows what she or he needs.

LOOKING IN THE CLASSROOM

Characteristics of the Prekindergarten Child

Ames and Ilg (1976) describe the four-year-old going on five as "Wild and Wonderful!" Children of this age have marvelous imaginations, must be physically active, say whatever comes to mind, often have extreme emotional reactions to situations, love to play with friends, sometimes experience difficult separation distress, and can suddenly become an angry or tearful two-year-old if tired or frightened. Teachers who can accept both the wild and the wonderful aspects of the preprimary child will be rewarded with a responsive classroom environment very much suited to the needs of the young child.

The Psychosocial Task of the Child

The four-year-old learns by doing and is not much concerned with learning complex things. Children of this age thoroughly enjoy actively experimenting and manipulating materials, but are usually disinterested in long explanations from teachers and parents. Erikson (1963) describes the preprimary child's psychosocial task as one of building initiative. Initiative is demonstrated in the child as a sense of purpose and makes the four-year-old easy to engage and eager to learn. Unbridled initiative can lead the young child to aggression against peers and teachers, or it can be expressed in verbal manipulation as, for instance, when a child says, "You aren't my friend!"

Teachers can help nurture initiative in children by clearly stating goals and expectations for them whenever possible. When faced with continued inappropriate behavior, teachers can restrict choices to only a few and then gradually increase choices as children begin to control behavior. Teachers can also support children by pointing out consequences of inappropriate behavior. "If you kick down their block structure, I will know that you should not play in the block corner again today."

Characteristics of Preoperational Thinking

The preprimary child's thought is characterized by egocentricity. Children see the world from their own point of view and have difficulty understanding someone else's perspective. They display their egocentric view during a game of hide and seek, for example, when they hide their head under a table and imagine that no one can see them.

In addition to egocentricity, the young child's thought is characterized by magical elements. Children believe that inanimate objects have human characteristics and intentions. When a child says, "My bike hurt me!" she means that the bike had the intention to hurt her. Young children think that it is possible for cloud shapes in the sky to be real and that the moon follows wherever the child goes because it chooses to do so. Given the vast difference between preoperational children's thinking and adult thinking, it is no surprise that children think rocks grow if you pinch them three times.

The child's thought is also tied to the way things look because he cannot reason logically yet. Children are forced to make judgments about experience based on their perception of reality. A preoperational child who is given two rows of eight pennies, where one row is stretched out, will say that there are now more pennies in the long row. This is true even when the child has counted each row and has stated that there are eight pennies in each. Young children think according to what they perceive is true. Unable to rely on logical reasoning, they rely on perception (Seefeldt 1984).

Understanding the unique way in which children think helps a teacher know what to teach. During circle time, one teacher asked her class of four-year-olds to vote on which story to read. After the votes were counted, she asked the children which was more, 19 or 6. One girl said 6 was more than 19. The teacher asked, "How do you know that?" The child explained that her sister was 6 (years old) and that 6 was more (old) than she was. From the child's point of view, this is quite an intelligent and reasonable answer. It certainly affects the kind of classroom activities teachers do with children. Unless young children are free to use open-ended materials in their own way and at their own pace, they will not be able to refine erroneous ideas.

If preoperational children are not certain that one object stands for one number when counting, then adding and subtracting exercises or worksheets are inappropriate for them. Instead, they should have a variety of play-oriented materials to explore and organize; open-ended activities such as blocks, water, sand, and art materials; and a housekeeping play area. Children should be free to choose what they want to do in the classroom, and there should be enough materials so that they can rotate from one to the other easily.

Types of Problem-Solving Activities

Once a teacher knows the characteristics of prekindergarten children, problem-solving activities will grow out of the play of the children and the natural life of the classroom, as well as out of activities created by the teacher. Not all problems continue to be interesting, and often young children lose interest before completing the activity. It is better for a child to find another activity of interest than to stay because the teacher desires her to complete the problem-solving process. Problem-solving activities take a large variety of forms. Let us take a closer look at the different kinds of problem-solving activities suggested by Goffin and Tull (1985).

Discussion Problems

One teacher decided to ask the children what could be done about disruptive gun fighting in the classroom. She began the discussion by asking if anyone could help solve the problem of some children running about and shooting other children. The most avid gun shooters immediately mumbled, "I didn't do it; it wasn't me!" It took some time to convince the children that the teacher was asking for opinions and would not punish anyone. One boy hesitantly explained that the guns were necessary for his play. The teacher asked if the shooting was all right with everyone. Several children said they were afraid of guns and did not want to be shot. The gun shooters said that they needed guns to fight the ghosts and bad guys. The teacher asked the children if there was a way that the ghosts could be shot without shooting the children. She wrote down what the children said and posted it on the bulletin board. These are some of the solutions the children suggested.

1. You can shoot the monsters, ghosts, and bad guys, but not the people.
2. You can shoot at the floor, ceiling, and walls and out

the window. (Unless a person is there!)

3. Can you shoot dolls? (A vote was needed for this.) No, because they look like people.
4. Can you shoot a real monster? Not unless you think it is real.
5. Can you pretend to shoot yourself? Yes, if you think it's O.K. No, if you don't!

Throughout the year the children referred to the gun rules chart when the occasion presented itself.

Interpersonal Problems

Problems related to everyday relationships are called interpersonal problems. In one classroom, three- and four-year-olds were playing in the housekeeping corner, making dinner and stirring soup. Suddenly a child from the block corner ran over and snatched a spoon right out from under a child's nose. The teacher helped the children see this incident as a problem to solve. The child who took the spoon explained that he needed one for his block game and the cooks had them all. The teacher then helped the children formulate alternatives. They decided that you cannot snatch the spoon, but you can ask for one or make one out of a toy like the scoops in the sand table. The children can take turns stirring and cooking so that there will be spoons left over for others to use. The two children involved decided to take turns. The children were quite happy to have worked out this problem to everyone's satisfaction.

Movement Problems

The following example of a movement problem involves children acting on objects. Four-year-olds constructed a track with paper towel rolls collected by the teacher. Two tracks were built so that each child could observe not only her own track, but her partner's as well. A basket with many balls of different sizes and weights was placed in between the two tracks. In addition, several wooden cubes were put in the basket.

Children began by seeing whose ball rolled the farthest. When one track seemed to have slower balls that did not roll as far, a child began to observe the track closely. The teacher asked what he wanted to do. "To make the balls go faster." The teacher asked, "How do you think you can change the track so that the ball will roll down faster?" The boy did not realize that his track had less of an incline. He decided to shore the entire track up off the floor with wooden blocks. This did not change the incline. With the help of friends he made sure the paper towel rolls were taped securely so that small balls could not roll out the side. He changed the balls he was using in case they were "slow" ones and discarded any cubes. Finally, he and his friends decided to take the wooden blocks out from under the track and lift the top of the track, thereby making a steeper incline. Balls then zoomed through the track!

Skill Problems

An example of skill problems occurred when the teacher put out an apple tree game in which the children had to roll dice and take the same number of apples off the tree. The game was over when all the apples were gone. At the end of the game, the children could not decide how to count so many apples. The teacher asked how they could figure out a way to move the apples so that they could be counted more easily. After many tests and predictions, the children found it easier to put all the felt apples around the edge of the table and count them in a row.

Strategy Problems

Using strategy problems with young children can be as simple as deciding how to spread butter on toast, how to clean up a paint spill, how to put one napkin at each place at the table, or how to count spaces on a board game to see if a child has moved more spaces than her friend. Open-ended art activities offer daily opportunities for children to experiment with making decisions and developing strategies for accomplishing goals. At Halloween, one prekindergarten child made a cat costume for herself out of construction paper, which she taped to the front of her dress. She discovered a problem when she tried to add a tail. She had trouble understanding where the tail should go. Does it go on the back of the costume? Then no one can see it. Does it go on the front of the costume? Cats don't have tails in front. After many trials and errors and collaboration with friends, she decided the best place for the tail was "on the back of me!"

LESSON PLANS: WEBBING

Most early childhood teachers in public schools are responsible for a variety of paperwork and record keeping tasks, which seems to increase each year. Lesson planning is one of the least popular responsibilities among teachers, and most find it tedious and not entirely useful. In a classroom with an integrated curriculum, planning can take a new and different approach from what was done in the past. Krogh (1990) and Bromley (1991) describe a new system of planning called *curriculum webbing*, which attempts to replicate the natural way that children learn in informal settings. Subject areas are combined to achieve a more natural experience, the way children learn on their own. A web can be created from a piece of children's literature or from a concept or topic. Each subject area is integrated with the others so that the children will have meaningful experiences that relate to their developmental level.

An example of how to plan using curriculum webbing, rather than day-by-day outlines of activities, begins with choosing a concept or book and then brainstorming with teachers about any related topics. After choosing a topic, the subject areas of the web (the radials) are filled in, and then the subject areas are integrated with other areas (Bromley 1991;

Krogh 1990; Katz & Chard 1989). How can the language curriculum, for example, be integrated with other subject areas? Children who play in the classroom and build social relationships do so by talking and communicating. These natural elements provide the basis for planning. Since the early childhood curriculum is no longer focused on building isolated skills what has taken its place? Language activities are in every area of the curriculum. The teacher now endeavors to create a print environment in the classroom. Teale and Sulzby (1986) describe the child as a developing reader/writer who experiences literacy everywhere in the classroom.

Listening, speaking, reading, and writing are a constant process for the children. In the block corner, they put signs on the garage; in the housekeeping corner, they take orders in their restaurant; at the art table, they dictate sentences about their artwork; during cooking activities, they try to figure out the recipe by reading the pictures and predicting what to do next. Language and math are integrated when the children figure out if there are enough snacks for everyone or how many letters are in a child's name or when they compare names to discover who has the longest name.

When a teacher begins planning with a project in mind, making a web helps to organize without being rigid. Curriculum webbing is a means of balancing subject areas in the curriculum. When a concept is integrated across the curriculum, the web may provide enough structure to eliminate the need for a chronological schedule of activities. On the other hand, it may help the teacher to make such an outline from the web.

The following is a planning web constructed by preprimary teachers in a university graduate class. The central or core idea for the web is "bread." Web strands are connected to the core and represent categories of information: for example, everyone eats bread, ingredients for making bread, nutrition and bread, stories and words about bread, ethnic breads, how grain is made into bread, and seeds and grains. Each web strand is supported by new information and details (Bromley 1991).

Ethnic bread, for example, might include the following strand supports: the kinds of breads you have eaten that are flat, the kinds of breadlike food that come from warm (cold) countries, the varieties of food that people put on bread, and your favorite kind of bread. In a preprimary class, the teacher might include some of the following activities from the "bread" web: Begin with a discussion about the different kinds of bread people eat, read and act out *The Gingerbread Man*, make biscuits, sing "The Muffin Man" and "Jimmy Crack Corn," and make a chart showing children's preferences for the different foods that can be put on muffins (butter, margarine, peanut butter, cheese, cream cheese, jelly, etc.).

Webs or maps like the one described above are flexible and should be constructed through a brainstorming session with all the teachers who are involved with the children. This may even include the children in the class or perhaps their parents. This kind of planning helps teachers adapt to the changing needs and interests of children. It is also a collaborative tool through which teachers, assistant teachers, and student teachers share in the planning process.

Chapter 5

FOR THE KINDERGARTEN TEACHER

PROFILE OF A TEACHER

Rita has been in her present suburban classroom for six years. Having taught in public schools for a total of 20 years, as well as having directed a preschool, she is an expert when it comes to the education of young children. She completed an M.Ed. in early childhood education and teaches evenings in the early childhood division of a local community college.

Rita characterizes her classroom as a hodgepodge of children from many cultures and economic levels. She sees this as a challenge and over the years has steadily moved toward individualization within the curriculum.

Problem solving is the essence of a good kindergarten program. It allows me to reach each child at his own level and assess the right time for specific learnings to occur. I can focus on the individual and his needs. Problem solving is the best way to infuse the subjects I am mandated to teach into the classroom curriculum. It allows children to figure answers out for themselves in an integrated way. It's easy to learn about children by watching them problem solve. I am a learner and I find it hard to understand other teachers who do not think of themselves in this same way. How can you teach without also learning?

I feel that I have come the full circle in allowing children to assume the responsibility for their own learning. Just as I am responsible for MY own learning, children, too, must be responsible for their learning. Years ago, I thought my main job was to pour all that knowledge into each little head. This was passive learning. Now I truly believe that I must trust a child, observe carefully to see what it is that the child needs, and provide for that need, allowing the child to learn in his own time at his own level. This is active learning.

My role has changed. For some children, I supply positive encouragement. For some children, I supply a special book about a special topic of interest, and for others, I give attention to and reinforcement of the learnings I observe. I set the stage for learning.

I strongly believe in parent education and know that the parent is the child's first teacher. I spent enormous amounts of my time helping parents understand how young children learn and what it is that they can do to promote this learning. I tell them to LOOK, WAIT, and LISTEN. LOOK at their child and keep good eye contact. WAIT for their child to talk, and LISTEN to what is being said. My time is well spent working with parents as they support what goes on in my classroom and strengthen the home/school connection that I believe is so important. Teaching is a trusting relationship between the child and the adult. Children learn in relationships. Problem solving in a multicultural classroom is especially important. I must provide the children of today with the ways to help make tomorrow better. Social relationships actually force problem solving each day in many different ways. Learning to get along with each other is hard, but problems can be solved. I want my children to learn from their experiences and to be able to apply that learning to future experiences.

LOOKING IN THE CLASSROOM

Rita's concern about providing problem-solving opportunities for children in a multicultural classroom is an important aspect of good early childhood practice. The multicultural curriculum, or the broader term *anti-bias curriculum,* is an approach to education values. The anti-bias curriculum emphasizes the positive concept that differences are healthy. In the past, teachers made great efforts to avoid stereotyping children by ignoring differences. Derman-Sparks and the A.B.C. Task Force (1989) explain that avoiding differences in children actually creates bias because it emphasizes "we" and "they" as separate categories. Multicultural education, then, values cultural pluralism. In this way, young children can share in the richness of diversity as a stepping stone in discovering the similarities in all human beings.

Addressing differences is a problem-solving exercise for children, and it does a great deal to help children broaden their view and find shared experiences that are enriching and empowering. Cultural diversity is a fact of daily life in the United States. Children continuously receive multicultural education, not only from the classroom, but also through family, peers, community groups, television, and videos. Sometimes these experiences are positive, and sometimes they are quite negative. In an educational setting, then, a multicultural perspective serves as a means for children to share in the fullness of our diverse American heritage.

Given this understanding, teachers find themselves with many questions concerning the multicultural curriculum. Why should we teach a multicultural curriculum when all the children in the class are the same race? It is unrealistic to think that the classroom should be isolated from the larger society. Dewey called the classroom a microcosm of society. The classroom should be a reflection of the pluralism of American society even if that racial or ethnic diversity is not represented in a specific classroom. The teacher's purpose is to create an environment in which children can develop an understanding of the shared experience of all people.

Early childhood teachers are also concerned that they find resources and materials that do not stereotype cultural and ethnic groups. Very often dolls, books, games, and other materials are highly stereotypic and depict a specific group of people in only one set way. Creating the anti-bias environment in a classroom begins with a careful examination of all the materials and decorations that children work with or see in the room. The classroom should be decorated with pictures of children and adults from major ethnic groups, of elderly as well as young people, of both men and women, and of people performing a variety of jobs. Pictures of nontypical or special children and adults should also be included. They should be represented as active and not dependent. All of these pictures should be about ordinary daily life.

Too often cultures are taught to children from the point of view of the past, and children cannot help but think about these cultures as if they were the same today. Native Americans are an example of such discrimination. In a kindergarten classroom, a teacher was trying to help children think more broadly about Native American peoples, and she asked the children how these people dressed today and what their homes were like. One child answered that she thought Indians would be cold since they wore only a cloth in front and back. Most children thought that Native Americans still lived in teepees. The children were astonished when the teacher invited another teacher who had a Native American background to visit the class. Some wondered how she could be Indian!

For children, it is not the information about different countries and cultures that is important. It is instead how *meaningful* the multicultural experience is for the children involved. A suburban kindergarten class was discussing the Spanish classes they were beginning the following week. One boy raised his hand and told the class that "the Spanish" all lived in Chicago. Rather than letting the opportunity for problem solving about differences go by, the teacher replied, "Yes, many Spanish families live in Chicago. In fact, I am Spanish and I live in Chicago. But there are also many Spanish families who live in all the towns where you live." The boy did not see how this could be true until a girl raised her hand and said that she lived in a different town and she was Spanish. Over several weeks, the children continued to ask the teacher about her Mexican heritage. On another occasion, the same boy asked the teacher something about her experience of being born in Mexico. The teacher explained that she was not born in Mexico; she was born in Chicago, but her parents were born in Mexico. This was a difficult problem to figure out until children began to relate these ideas to their own families and relatives. Children began to think about relatives from other countries, and these discussions led to a long study of the differences and similarities of family life among children in the class.

It is important for teachers to understand that a multicultural curriculum must conform to the tenents of good developmental practice in the same way that any other part of the curriculum does. Kindergarten children still need an active learning approach and activities and experiences that are integrated across the curriculum, rather than tacked onto the curriculum. Many anti-bias problem-solving opportunities grow out of the natural life of the classroom and can become extended projects to study, as in the family example given above. Derman-Sparks and the A.B.C. Task Force (1989) refer to the usual practice of teachers who try to expose children to other cultures by "visiting" other countries. Teachers plan to share food, clothing, and music, but only on holidays or for a day during the year. This is described as trivializing another culture. Children can learn only stereotypes in this way. To avoid trivializing, children need to be helped with positive and appropriate responses to differences throughout the year. One kindergarten teacher used Japanese newspapers for the art table, for special projects, and to line the rabbit cage. She borrowed Japanese children's books and put them on the shelf. After several weeks children began to notice the different printing and asked the teacher about it. When the children asked the teacher to read a Japanese book, she explained that she could not and asked if they knew anyone who could read it. The children decided to invite a Japanese parent in the school to visit the class and read the books. Eventually this shared reading became a regular practice throughout the year.

The most important element in an effective multicultural program is the sensitivity of the teacher to culture and diversity. Teachers have a critical influence on what children understand about their world and themselves. For a successful educational program, the teacher must have a positive attitude concerning differences. Children are very much aware of the insincerity of teachers. Studies of teacher expectations found that teachers communicate both motivating and limiting messages indirectly to children, coloring self-perceptions and attitudes (Saracho & Spodek 1983). Children learn, for example, that nonstandard English is deficient when teachers reject language that is not "standard English." How can correct language usage be taught? By accepting the child as she is and then working through the language differences over time.

The benefits of a multicultural perspective are many for children. They develop a healthy self-esteem and pride in who they are, as well as increased social awareness. Each child develops to his or her potential. Multicultural experiences are another way for children to develop critical thinking. Understanding differences has to do with pursuing knowledge and looking for answers. Derman-Sparks (1989) explains the goals of an anti-bias curriculum as enabling children to build confidence and identity, to increase language and problem-solving skills, and to develop an empathic view of others.

LESSON PLANS: PROJECTS

As children strive to make sense out of their world and learn, teachers endeavor to plan programs that meet the children's holistic needs. One rather new curriculum-planning design is described by Katz and Chard (1989) as the project approach. Projects grow out of the interests and needs of the individuals in a classroom. This approach encourages children to ask questions and seek answers and to collaborate with peers. When several children or the whole class undertakes a project, they study a topic in some depth over a period of time. Depending on the children's interest, their ages, and the nature of the topic, a project could last from several days to many weeks. Kindergarten children are more likely to sustain interest in a project for longer periods than younger children are. Projects to be explored might include "how our school works," "going shopping," "our weather," "studying a nearby construction site.

The work children do on a project is not intended to replace the entire curriculum, but as a major part of the program, projects encourage children to develop emergent skills across the subject areas of the curriculum. Project work takes a good deal of prior and ongoing planning on the part of the children and the teacher and should complement the spontaneous experiences from which children learn a great deal. The project approach, though guided by the teacher, must be a reciprocal process with the children in order to be effective. Because of this, projects are free-flowing and somewhat unstructured.

Projects begin with a decision about what topic to choose. Individual teachers can select a topic, or this can be done by the children with the help of the teacher. Sometimes schoolwide topics are chosen by teachers, and sometimes topics are mandated by school systems. In any case, the way that the children undertake the work of a project is always unique to the individuals in the group.

Once the topic is chosen, teachers need to establish the key ideas involved in the topic. If the topic is the weather, for example, the teachers should brainstorm as many ideas as possible about the concepts that topic comprises. The topic is then written in the center of a sheet of paper. At this point, brainstorming ideas are webbed together so that major ideas radiate from the center topic and subheadings flow from the minor topics. After the initial work is completed, another list can be made that connects the project into subject areas.

The project approach was undertaken in an elementary school in which teachers decided that the topic for the year would be "how things work." The kindergarten teacher worked out a project with her children that was entitled, "how our school works." Most of the kindergarten children in the class were unaware of where offices and people were located in the school. In the first phase of the project, children decided to draw pictures and invent the spelling for the places and people with whom they were most familiar, their own classroom and teacher, the classroom next door, the library, and the cafeteria. The children then decided they should take a trip around the school to find out what other rooms were in the school. They discovered the gym and pool, the principal's office, a post office, a mail room for teachers, and the elementary playground. All of these places were drawn, measured, discussed, written about, and negotiated by the children on a daily basis over a period of three weeks.

In the second phase of the project, the children decided to interview the important people in the school and create representations of them. The children created marvelous depictions of the man in the cafeteria who gives children milk, the woman in the maintenance office who showed the children the boiler room, the nurse who gives children bandaids, and many other people who meant something special to the children. In the course of the project, the children discussed the differences in people: some had different skin colors, spoke with different accents, or were different ages. The children learned a great deal about their school, about diversity, about working together, and about mathematics, literacy, art, science, and social studies. For this classroom, the project approach to planning was successful in encouraging the children to think more broadly, and it challenged them to stretch their ideas.

Chapter 6

FOR THE FIRST GRADE TEACHER

PROFILE OF A TEACHER

Erik, a first-year teacher, has been hired by a large school system to teach in an inner-city school. The building is very old, and his classroom has not been used for the past five years. Erik arrived on the first day to find no supplies, no equipment, and a room in need of serious cleaning.

Right from the start the children and I began to use problem solving. I feel strongly about helping children develop an ownership in their learning so I saw this situation as an opportunity to help children become actively involved in taking charge. I asked the children what kind of a room they wanted to have this school year and we talked, made lists, and negotiated ideas. We voted and decided on solutions to the many problems the setting had established. We talked about class rules and negotiated beginning rules.

Problem solving was new to my children and I had to model a lot in the beginning. By the time we had organized the physical environment, decided the structure and rules for the learning environment, and discussed interests and needs for the year, the children were quite familiar with problem solving and had, in fact, begun to use strategies for solving social problems without my help. I think using problem solving right from the start set the tone for the year—the children felt involved and invested in their own learning because they were in control. Problem solving allows children to be in control. They decided what they wanted and were reponsible for the choices they made. The children were proud of their room and proud of the learning that took place there.

Actually, not having the standard supplies and equipment allowed us to establish a more hands-on environment than I saw in other classrooms in the school. We used tables to seat groups of four students instead of individual desks. This one change facilitated more cooperative and prosocial relationships than I had seen during my student teaching experience. Because limited art supplies were available, we often thought of new ways to use the supplies. For instance, we used newspaper as a bulletin board background material. By the end of the school year, I saw children reading the background print on the boards as well as the displayed print. Using newspaper, because it was readily available and cheap, actually increased the reading skills of my students!

Probably the most exciting part of the year was watching problem solving "feed on itself." By this I mean, the more problem solving we did, the better the children became at it. As they used problem solving effectively, they used it more often. It kind of fed on itself, growing and changing as the year went along. The children became very good at listening to others, generating creative and interesting solutions, and negotiating terms. Their communication skills improved and I saw a group cohesiveness develop. This togetherness was important because often our classroom curriculum was different from the others in the school. The children needed to be able to support each other and present a united front. I saw the children become better at evaluating and this, in turn, helped in their everyday work. They became more independent and self-corrected their own work. They didn't have to come to me to get the right answer. Their self-esteem improved as they developed competence.

Through a room newsletter that I began and eventually, as the year progressed, the children took over, parents were included in the problem-solving process. Rather than talk in terms of what I did, I promoted what the children and I had done together. Sometimes I would include the ideas that were generated during problem solving. I would include the voting totals so that the parents became aware of the part each child played in establishing our classroom. We SHARED with parents and, by sharing, enlisted their aid. Sometimes I would relate the step-by-step technique we used to solve a problem and I always used the terms "problem" and "solution." Sometimes I would include sample questions that parents could ask children to encourage expanded thinking. "How did you do that?" "What would happen if. . .?" "What is another way you could do that?" These are questions that I often ask in the classroom and now I hear the children asking each other these same questions.

I think it is important to help parents and children speak the same language when talking about what is going on at school. I want to make parent/child communications as easy and as understandable as possible. This helps me as the teacher. Problem solving has helped me as the teacher.

LOOKING IN THE CLASSROOM

The best first grade classroom is not first grade *at all,* but rather a multigrade group of children above, at, and below the typical age of the first grade child. In the same ways that a multicultural grouping within a classroom naturally provides diversity and an exchanging of a variety of ideas, a multigrade classroom provides a productive atmosphere for the rapidly changing rates and levels of learning that occur in young children. According to Bredekamp in *Developmentally Appropriate Practice* (1987), teachers should plan a curriculum that is, first, appropriate for the developmental level of the child and, second, appropriate for the individual. This is easier to do in a multigrade classroom. One of the best features of using the problem-solving process is that it allows children to respond at a variety of developmental levels and in individual ways. In fact, children are *encouraged* to respond at various levels and in various unique ways.

Scheduling large blocks of time allows children to plan, participate, and evaluate learnings. This facilitates integrated learning. Children do not just learn about reading, then close off that part of their brain and learn about mathematics, and then close off that part of their brain and learn about writing. All parts of learning are integrated, and the best teaching presents ideas in integrated ways. A typical large-time-block schedule might look like this:

9:00 Opening Greetings and Daily Organizational Tasks
9:15 Language Arts

This would include a variety of activities, such as writing in journals and keeping word files; using "transitional" (often called "inventive") spelling to record ideas; reading individual books from a classroom collection offering a wide selection of topics, types, and levels, ranging from picture books to literature;

talking with others about reading and writing; planning and initiating dramas; and listening to stories written by classmates. (Books about using this whole language method include many ideas as starters for classroom teachers.) In essence, this large time period is to be spent allowing children to investigate any and all of the language arts. This investigation may also lead to exploring mathematics, science, art, and music ideas. Sometimes this activity will be done individually; and sometimes in small groups. Solving problems during this time is a part of the learning process.

10:45 Outside Physical Activities
11:15 Large-Group Storytime
11:45 Music and Movement Activities
12:00 Lunch
 1:00 Large-Group Discussion

This time might include group instruction, discussions of skills, evaluation of morning activities, introduction of new materials, social problem solving, etc.

1:30 Learning Centers

Hands-on activities for individuals or small groups are investigated. This might include mathematics activities, such as estimating and matching. Science activities might include measuring and cooking. Art activities might include painting and printing. Puzzles and manipulatives would be permanent parts of learning centers. The interests and needs of the children set the focus of the centers and also dictate the materials and directions of the learnings.

2:30 Large-Group Time

During this time, the day is evaluated and goals for the next day are reset. The children are encouraged to share experiences and learnings with each other.

3:00 Dismissal

A simple schedule such as this affords the classroom teacher the opportunity to promote integrated learning, choices, and problem solving during the full school day. By joining subject areas such as reading, mathematics, science, and art, the individual learner can investigate and explore many varieties of ideas in many meaningful ways.

Using a *unit* approach to help organize learning is one way a teacher can incorporate individual ideas into a set curriculum from a school district. Here is an example of how a large-time-block schedule can be combined with set curricular goals and individual needs using problem solving within a classroom.

Cathy brought snapshots of her newly born kitten to class one day. During sharing time at the close of the day, all of the children had an opportunity to look at the pictures and comment. Many related similar experiences about kittens, newly born pets, and other household animals. The teacher, recognizing this as a common interest of most of the children, asked if the class would like to learn more about pets. The children agreed. Time was set aside to talk about this some more on the next day. (By giving the children time overnight to think about their own experiences, the teacher allowed each child an opportunity to formulate ideas and plan for learning.)

The following day the teacher had prepared the classroom by providing books and puppets of different pets. Photographs of many kinds of families with many kinds of pets had been placed around the room. Paint and paper were available in an art center. Tapes of animal sounds were available in a listening corner. A poem about a kitten was printed on the board. The teacher had provided the space and materials to begin the investigation of the topic.

During the first large block of time, the children began to gather in small groups to use the books and materials. Two sat together to share a picture book about kittens. They cooperated as they verbalized the text to go along with the pictures on each page. As they finished the book, they decided to make a book of their own. The teacher asked, "What do you need to do to make your own book?" The children decided to make a list of things they needed to do. (This is problem solving.) Using transitional spelling (spelling words as they sound),they completed the list. The children decided that one would draw the pictures and the other would write the words. Their work began.

In another part of the room, three children began playing with the puppets. One left the group to look closer at the variety of pictures around the room.

Carlos: Look at this family with their pet.

Djaune: That is what this animal is. (He pointed to the puppet he held in his hand.)

Carlos: Let's pretend that we are this family and this is our dog.

Jessica: We can make hats to wear just like the boys in this picture.

Djaune: I've never seen hats like those. How will we make them?

And so the problem was identified and the process began.

Sometimes the teacher leads the children into thinking about various aspects of problem solving; sometimes the children begin the process all by themselves. But it *is* the teacher's responsibility to create the environment that supports and encourages problem solving. This teacher provided time, space, and materials. This teacher also trusted the children to be able to find learnings that were important to them within the environment that was provided.

Ramsey (1987) uses a pet unit for young children as an example of how multicultural education should be woven into the curriculum. The following activities and topics are included:

Caring for pets: social responsibility
Cooperative care of a class pet

Similarities among all pets
Diversity of pets
Learning about pets belonging to people in the classroom
Friendships between people and pets, despite differences
Names of animals in other languages
Pets in other places
Communicating with pets
Protecting the rights of pets (p.7)

A further investigation of pets might include the follow
activities and learnings using a problem-solving process.

Writing

- Keeping a journal when caring for a personal and/or class pet
- Making a grocery list of the food needed for a pet
- Listing kinds of pets
- Sending an inquiry letter to a pet store

Listening

- Identifying sounds of different pets
- Hearing stories about pets from classmates

Reading

- Making up a story to go along with pictures in a book
- Planning and designing an original book about pets
- Practicing an oral poetry reading with others in a group
- Formulating a KWL chart (see Chapter 3)
- Listing information gained through reading about pets

Drama

- Acting out a story from a book
- Negotiating parts in a play
- Participating in a drama production

Mathematics

- Estimating food amounts needed for the care of a pet
- Graphing and comparing sizes of pets
- Counting and comparing pets within family units
- Matching pets with accessories (one to one)
- Using a calendar to record data
- Sorting pets by sizes

Science

- Comparing ideas on similarities and differences of living things
- Investigating food and shelter for pets
- Observing habits of pets
- Cooking dog biscuits

Art

- Designing posters about pets
- Drawing pets
- Illustrating books and poetry
- Viewing representations of pets of various cultures
- Looking for similar lines and forms in pets
- Comparing pets in famous paintings

Social Studies

- Sharing responsibilities of caring for classroom pets
- Taking turns
- Deciding rules
- Considering the roles of pets
- Considering the rights of pets

Music and Movement

- Imitating animal movements
- Comparing pets to different kinds of music

Often teachers think that curriculum goals set by the school district must be followed and taught as listed in the guide. Most curriculum goals established by school districts for a first grade child can be met by exploring this unit. The difference is that the teacher considered the interests and needs of the children and organized the teaching around a unit plan, including the goals in a meaningful and interesting format. By using a central focus, the teacher includes the children at all levels of learning. Here are some goals listed from a typical first grade curriculum guide.

- Obtaining information from visual aids
- Drawing conclusions
- Identifying details
- Making predictions
- Recognizing cause and effect
- Speaking clearly
- Participating in choral readings
- Dramatizing main characters
- Reading to enjoy
- Reading for information
- Using standard English
- Learning about other cultures
- Beginning to use written words to communicate
- Demonstrating a use for measurement
- Identifying the days of the week
- Cooperating on projects
- Sharing information
- Using observation as a basis for judgments
- Collecting, recording, and interpreting information
- Predicting outcomes
- Acquiring confidence in using mathematics
- *Solving Problems*

Each one of these goals was reached in the activities included in the unit about pets.

Look carefully at your curriculum goals, think about the interests and needs of the children in your class, and begin planning units using large blocks of time. By trusting the children to formulate answers to their own problems, you can guide and encourage good learning practices in your classroom.

LESSON PLANS: UNITS

Many books include activities that can be included in lesson plans to help children develop problem-solving skills. *Living and Learning with Children* by Paula Jorde-Bloom (1989) has many activities that are appropriate for a hands-on curriculum based on problem solving. It is important to remember that the emphasis of the lesson must be on what the child is interested in learning. Buying and using an activity book simply to find ways to fill up the hours of the school day is unproductive and leads to fragmented learning for the children. Good learning activities must grow out of the needs and interests of the children within the classroom. Good learning is integrated and allows the children to choose what is best for them.

Problem solving is more than activities. It is a basic philosophy that encourages each child to assume the responsibility, with the teacher's support, for the learning that occurs. *Any* activity within the classroom curriculum can be approached from a problem-solving point of view. The teacher does not *tell* the children what to do, but rather explores options with the children. The teacher does not *assign* tasks, but rather encourages the children to make choices. The teacher does not *generate* questions with only one answer, but rather encourages a variety of creative solutions. It is a problem-solving approach that sets the tone for the young child's learning.

Here is a lesson plan for the language arts block of the pet unit. Be aware that planning for young children can be done on a general weekly basis, but must be refined each day as the group sets new objectives and as new learnings occur. The responsibility of the teacher is to keep track of each child's progress and to help each child set new challenges and practice skills.

Monday

- Work with small groups in organizing pet unit (KWL chart)
- Provide new books and puppets
- Help group children for unit work

Tuesday

- Begin a board list of vocabulary words using transitional spelling provided by the children
- Check supplies for individual word collections
- Gather children interested in writing a group story; transcribe their dictations and decide on a method of keeping a copy
- Observe children using puppets and take notes on oral language abilities

Wednesday

- Work with children writing kitten book (Make a list? Draw pictures?)
- Provide a book of ideas on animal costumes for group working on play; help them plan workable costumes and identify and gather needed materials
- Monitor group sharing stories they read (evaluate progression and level of skills)
- Find children interested in making copies of dog biscuit recipe for use in cooking center (How else can this be done?)

There is no doubt that planning for learning that grows out of the needs and interests of each child is more difficult than following teacher-directed learning plans. Innovative ideas should be listed and then extended and expanded as the learning progresses. As you can see from the example included, lesson plans for child-centered learnings almost become jotted notes of directions to go and possibilities to discover for the teacher and the children. Often teachers must add new plans and eliminate unused plans daily, while continuing to move toward general learning goals. Fortunately, planning in this way improves as teachers practice the skill. Do not be discouraged if this kind of planning is new to you—it does get better and easier as you practice the skill more often.

Evaluation from this kind of planning is individual and requires much self-reflection on the part of the teacher. The interactive process is energizing and, when including the children, can be an important part of a shared learning experience within the classroom.

Chapter 7

FOR THE SECOND GRADE TEACHER

PROFILE OF A TEACHER

Linda has been a second grade teacher for 25 years. She has served on district curriculum committees, has been active in professional groups that advocate for young children, and has taken many hours of graduate education courses. Active within the community, she has watched the school population change over the years. Linda *knows* second graders.

The pressures today on families are enormous. The family unit is being pulled in all directions, and the children are caught in the middle. The evils of society such as drugs and violence can't help but impact families and, just at a time when families need to draw in closer to protect one another, economic strains dictate that the adults spend more time at work to financially support the family unit. Times are hard, and I worry about the future of my children.

Over the years my teaching has changed. I value life skills being practiced in the classroom more than I did years ago. Yes, reading is important. Yes, mathematics is important. But the bottom line is that problem solving, decision-making, and making good choices are critical to the very survival of children. I believe that it is more important to promote skills in these areas during the school day because this learning goes across the curriculum. Problem solving is used in becoming a good reader. Problem solving is the basis for good mathematics skills. Problem solving is the CORE of my curriculum. It is used in every part of life, at every stage in life, and I include it in every part of my teaching.

I try to establish a classroom where children are free to try out new ideas. I want them to know that each idea they have is worthwhile and that others are listening. Beginning second graders are still very self-centered. Providing a classroom atmosphere where the ideas of others are valued takes lots of time, effort, and patience. Children have to feel confident about themselves before they can relate well to others. Problem solving provides the structure and a forum for an exchange of ideas. Problem solving helps children become independent.

LOOKING IN THE CLASSROOM

This is a busy and productive classroom. The individual desks are arranged in groups of three, and the children are talking to each other as they work in all parts of the room. Some of the windowsills have boxes filled with art materials. Books are located in three or four places around the room and seem to be grouped by subject matter. One part of the room has been turned into a writing center; another has a cardboard stage front for drama and has paper costumes nearby. Even the classroom bulletin boards have been organized by the children. A graph shows the work of five children, and on a table, manipulatives are sorted into groups of ten with labels by children. It is difficult to find the teacher amid the buzz of activity in the room.

In this classroom, children increase their skills individually. Reading and mathematics are contracted individually, and each student keeps track of his own progress. Each afternoon, small groups of children come together with the teacher to share ideas and/or problems they have encountered. Membership in these groups shifts as the ideas and/or problems change over the school year. As communication skills are integrated within the curriculum, sometimes the focus of the meeting is reading, sometimes mathematics, and sometimes writing, listening, or speaking. The focus depends on the needs of the children. Often the children share their own productions—stories, drama, poetry. This is an active learning environment.

The teacher understands and supports the value of encouraging children to listen to others and to discuss ideas. Each child is allowed to be a valued member of the group, no matter what level of skill she possesses. For example, Iris is able to make inferences from her readings, but Mary Jane is still struggling with understanding what the main idea is in each paragraph she reads. During the small-group time, the teacher is able to pair the two on a writing project they are both interested in and will observe carefully to see if Mary Jane is able to progress in her skills through the writing they do together. The teacher may, in fact, need to do some individual work with Mary Jane, but decides to try some peer cooperative work first. Perhaps being part of a team that is designing bulletin boards will help clarify what a main idea is. The teacher jots down some activities that may help Mary Jane—these activities are not all reading activities, but rather they use a variety of resources within the classroom. The teacher and Mary Jane have a conference.

T: You seemed to have trouble understanding the story you were reading today. What do you think is the problem?

M.J.: I didn't understand what all the ideas meant. I mean, what was the most important idea?

T: Yes, I thought that was the problem. I found some other books that you might read to help you understand better. Iris is working on a writing project and that work might help you. Can you think of some other ways to solve the problem?

M.J.: You and I could read a book together. Or maybe Bill could read with me. He seems to know all about this.

T: Those are good ideas. Some of the children are working on a bulletin board and have to figure out a good title for each of the sections of the board. You could decide to work with them. Tonight, at home, think about all the choices we have talked about. Maybe you will think of some other ideas. Tomorrow you can plan what you want to do and begin your work. We can set a time when we want to check to see how you are doing on your plan.

Individual problem solving helped this child identify needs and generate solutions, and it gave her time to focus on solutions. Evaluation of the results is an important part of the process. Because the teacher has organized the learnings within the classroom into an activity-based cooperative system, the teacher has time to help each child individually. Actually, in practice, most of the learning that occurs within the classroom is small-group—not individual—learning. The children tend to group themselves according to interests and needs. These groups are flexible. Occasionally the teacher will assess a child as needing skills that are being accumulated by a specific group of children and will suggest that the child should join that group. It is the combination of integrated subject matter and cooperative learning strategies that makes problem solving so important to young children. The ability to learn and practice strategies in meaningful situations makes the difference.

The children in a second grade classroom in Illinois discussed ecology one afternoon. From this discussion came an interest in improving the environment. Using a KWL method of investigation (see Chapter 3), the teacher helped the children focus on a specific ecology issue. The children wanted to know about garbage: Where did it come from? Where did it go? What happened to it? What could they do to help their community plan for the future?

The children in this class came from a wide range of economic and social strata. Many different ethnic groups and life styles were represented in the class. The teacher seized the opportunity to investigate this topic as a forum for practicing problem solving and exploring choices in a practical way. Some of the activities the children planned and initiated were as follows:

- Exchanging information about life styles (disposable products families use)
- Estimating the amount of plastic, aluminum, and paper garbage per week in each household
- Graphing each family member's use of throwaway items for one month
- Making a list of ways families could have less garbage
- Writing a letter to a local store asking that bulk items be stocked
- Experimenting with buried garbage items to see how long it takes them to decompose
- Writing poems about garbage and submitting them to the school newspaper
- Visiting a local recycling center
- Collecting local newspaper stories for a bulletin board display
- Keeping track of room garbage
- Interviewing the school janitor to see what happens to school garbage
- Writing projections about future societies
- Listing innovative ideas about product packaging
- Formulating new packages for products
- Initiating a school awareness campaign
- Developing individual vocabulary lists
- Considering cultural life styles and practices
- Writing original stories
- Reading materials about waste control
- Sharing information
- Establishing a measuring center to measure,

record, and compare aspects of garbage (tons, feet, lbs., etc.)
- Inventing recipes to use all possible food products
- Diagramming food chains
- Reporting on waste management procedures in the past

This investigation continued for three weeks and resulted in increased knowledge and skills in all subject areas of the curriculum. It provided the children with a better understanding of each other and waste management. This investigation *was* the curriculum—it was not "tacked on," but was instead the vehicle through which learning took place. The children were able to make choices, pursue interests, practice skills, and learn new skills all within the context of the investigation. This is the way young children learn. It is meaningful, it is interesting, and it is real.

The progress of each child is assessed in a variety of ways. The teacher asked each child to keep a file of his work. Periodically the teacher and the child look over the materials collected together and talk. By discussing the work with the child, the teacher is able to evaluate the progress made and help the child set new goals. Self-evaluation is also valued, and the teacher often asks the child to comment on the learnings that have occurred. The most valued means of assessment is observation. The teacher keeps a separate file for each child. Here the teacher places notes and comments based on observations. This combination of a variety of evaluative sources gives the teacher a more complete and clear picture of a child's progress than a paper-and-pencil test does.

Problem solving allows children to set goals and move down the avenues of learning. Problem solving encourages creativity and cooperation and fosters a sense of community necessary for the world of today and for the world of tomorrow.

LESSON PLANS: INDIVIDUALIZED LEARNING

By carefully listening to and observing the interests and needs of the children, the teacher can plan ahead. This allows the teacher to organize the learning and focus on appropriate ways to initiate learning. For instance, plans would include a variety of ways in which to incorporate learnings into lessons while problem solving. Some lessons may focus on listening, some on reading, and some on mathematics skills. It is the responsibility of the teacher to provide the children with the best forum for learning and to include a variety of ways to learn. Not all learning should come from listening or from reading. It is the teacher's responsibility to provide the balance and to meet the needs of all the learners within the group. By carefully planning, teachers can consider the learning styles of the children and provide for education.

A lesson plan for one part of the ecology study is included. Weekly planning may or may not be appropriate for your classroom. This plan is an example of a single mathematics lesson. Be sure to look at the other types of plans included at the ends of Chapters 4 through 8. It is important to follow some kind of plan if problem solving is to occur on a regular basis in the classroom. Planning helps the teacher organize thoughts and set goals and gives each lesson a direction. Evaluating the lesson will help measure the progress made by individuals, keep the lessons moving toward the goals, and encourage the teacher to find new methods and/or repeat those methods that are working with students. A possible lesson plan for one part of the ecology study previously discussed follows.

Date: Friday, November 16   *Time Needed: 1 hour*

ACTIVITY: Measuring Garbage

WHAT LEARNING I WANT TO EVALUATE

1. Cooperation within small groups
2. Investigation of nonstandard units of measurement
3. Oral communication skills
4. Discovery of relationship of parts to whole

LESSON PREPARATION

Provide rulers, two or three kinds of scales, yardsticks, tape measures, and lots of space. Markers, large paper for recording, crayons, and board space may be needed.

BEGINNINGS

Review garbage studies of the past week.

Ask:

- How do we know we have too much garbage in our community?
- How can we find out how much we have collected in our room this week? Encourage the children to list ways on the board for all to see
- How can we organize this project? Give help if needed as small groups are formed. Provide resources and assistance in physically moving bags and dividing materials

LESSON

Encourage the children to work in small groups to measure garbage. Provide limited measuring instruments so some groups will have to think of other ways to measure. Encourage groups to try out their ideas and record the measurements they take. Some may want to graph; if others want to follow that idea, then the graphs can be compared. Ask questions such as these:

- How many milk jugs are there end to end in a yard?
- Guess how much that will weigh?
- What weighs the most?
- Using the edge of your book to measure, how high is that stack of papers?

Encourage the children to use new units of measurement and to extend their learnings and share with other groups.

Close the lesson with a sharing time, and ask the children to estimate over the weekend how much garbage they will have at home on Saturday, using the units of measurement that they discovered today. (Monday this information will be shared and compared.)

EVALUATION

Take notes on—

Self:

1. Use of space and materials (for future planning)
2. Further extension of this activity
3. Reinforcement of understanding of parts-to-whole relationships

Child:

1. Individual oral language skills
2. Cooperation between children and between groups
3. Understanding of units of measurement (Who needs more help?)

A good lesson plan sets goals, has hands-on activity to ensure active learning, and includes self-evaluation (to improve teaching) and student evaluation (to improve learning). A good lesson provides problem solving.

Chapter 8

FOR THE THIRD GRADE TEACHER

PROFILE OF A TEACHER

Nancy has taught young children for 14 years in both private and public schools in and outside the United States. She has been in her present situation six years. Her class is about 50 percent regular third graders and 50 percent district-identified gifted and talented students. Nancy has had special training provided by her district in gifted and talented education.

I want all my children to think on their own. I want them to figure things out and use the knowledge they have. My job is to make them feel secure in experimenting with new ideas and new ways to do things. Making good small judgments leads to making good big judgments. This is what problem solving is all about. I want to make sure my children are prepared to make the best choice as they move through life.

Cooperative learning is an important part of the curriculum in this class. I never promote what I don't want to happen in my class. For example, I never divide the class by girls and boys as I don't want to promote the differences between the sexes. I want my children to see each other as individuals with worthwhile traits and traditions that must be respected. I model this respect for the class, and my expectations that each child will follow my example are high. By doing lots of group work, children learn to communicate and negotiate. They notice the contributions of each member of the group. They begin to understand that there are many different solutions to a problem because we all look at problems differently and that this is O.K. They learn to share and to work together. They learn to listen to each other and to compromise. These are all skills we need to get through life, and I want my children to start practicing these skills early.

I know that using problem solving as the basis for my curriculum is the best way to get and keep children excited about learning. Children learn by doing, and they especially learn from their mistakes. My role as the teacher is to have the confidence to turn them loose with their ideas and let them explore the possibilities. I let them do it themselves. Sometimes I will suggest that they use a peer as a resource. I think this promotes the closeness and interdependency within the group. Often I model mistakes, and I usually do not give answers. I want each child to feel the confidence that comes with being an independent learner.

Helping parents to help children is a very individual and customized process. By the time a child is eight, the pattern of parenting is pretty well set. Often I just help a parent step back and let the child establish independence. When I talk with parents I listen, communicate, negotiate, and generally model all the skills I am helping the children learn in my class. Then, as I do with children, I remind parents of the process we have worked through and ask them to try doing that with their own child. It works. Parents begin to see their child as a group member (of the family) with worthwhile contributions to be made. Problem solving as the learning process for parents and children helps make working together easier.

LOOKING IN THE CLASSROOM

A third grade classroom is more sophisticated than other early childhood classrooms. Children are generally able to focus on goals and carry through projects with ease. They are able to use resources well and know a great deal about the world around them. Interests are well defined and children look for learnings that are detailed and specific. Because of the developmental levels of the children and their varied interests, the classroom becomes a meshing place for ideas and discussions of a much wider range than before. Children's interests have usually moved out of the family unit into community and/or world affairs.

Social problem solving takes on an added importance in the third grade classroom. Learning conflict resolution skills, negotiation skills, and prosocial skills becomes an important part of the curriculum, as children develop independence.

In a third grade classroom in Washington State, children became involved with the following community actions, employing a variety of problem-solving strategies and techniques as the year progressed.

Big Brother/Big Sister roles

Discussion began by stating a school problem. Three children in the first grade were having trouble with older children harassing them on the way to school. A small group within the third grade classroom decided to become Big Brothers/Big Sisters to the younger children and assist them. This initial involvement spread to others in the class who also wanted to aid the younger children in some way. Ideas were explored, and a variety of solutions were offered. Some children began using extra time in school to assist younger children in keeping journals and diaries. Some children used recess time to assist younger children in developing motor skills. Some children wrote stories that they read to the younger children during a library period. Solutions to the problem were varied and met the needs of both the older and the younger students. A Big Brother/Big Sister Program was established within the third grade classroom. A formal meeting time was established weekly to discuss problems and graph solutions. Often the solutions were voted on before they were tried. Problem solving was used in a relevant and meaningful way to develop social responsibility within the third graders.

Pen Pals

The teacher brought a letter from a friend in the Peace Corps to class one day. She shared the letter with the children during the closing time at the end of the day. The children began to ask questions about the country. It was decided to set aside time the following morning to further discuss and formulate ideas. The next day the children came to school with lots of ideas. Using a KWL chart (see Chapter 3), information and ideas were sorted and categorized by the teacher and the children. A goal was set to learn more about the country in a variety of ways. One committee established by the class researched the country at the school library, one group searched through old National Geographic magazines for information, and one committee wrote back to the teacher's friend and asked for information on overseas pen pals. A month later a letter arrived with the name of a school willing to participate. The children met again to discuss further plans; established committees to find out about postal regulations and about local customs and traditions; and wrote the initial letters. Over the year, the pen pal project proved to be fruitful and ended with an exploration of photography (snapshots were sent), cooking (recipes were exchanged), and a comparison of school programs and rules. Extensive map work was included in the project, as was a close examination of individual customs, history, and traditions.

A UNICEF Fund-Raising Event

When a class member related to others a visit to a UNICEF store in Albuquerque, a few of the children wanted more information about this organization. Some went to the library to investigate, and others came together as a group to write a letter to the United Nations headquarters in New York. Acting on the initial information from the library, the children discussed and voted to support UNICEF and participate in some way. They decided to wait until more detailed information arrived from UNICEF and the project was tabled. Later that month the awaited letter arrived, along with a packet for neighborhood collections. The children came together and discussed this method of support, but decided to initiate their own ideas for a support project. During the following few weeks, they had lively exchanges of ideas—some workable and some not. The open exchange of ideas and acceptance of each class member as being important and worthwhile served to bond the children together. Three ideas were voted to be worth pursuing.

1. One group volunteered to write original stories about children in other countries, to illustrate these stories, and to "publish" the books. They would be sold at the school book fair in the winter. An assembly line process was discussed for the book production, roles and responsibililities were decided, and the work began. Within this group, problem solving occurred as the work progressed.

2. Another group decided to make a ball toss game that could be used at the school fun fair in the spring. The money spent by players would be donated to UNICEF. Drawings were made, and the game rules were negotiated. A list was made of needed supplies, and possible sources for materials were discussed.

3. The third group voted to make a video about UNICEF that would be used to solicit funds from community groups. They outlined the script and made arrangements to use the school video recorder. The video production required a story board: drawings of the sequencing of the appeal. Operating the video recorder required trial-and-error manipulation of the actual object before the problem was solved. The children investigated how a video recorder works and made time calculations through division and multiplication.

Each of these community actions was different; each began with creative ideas and involved a variety of problem-solving strategies. Skills and knowledge were learned during the year, but, even more important, the prosocial skills practiced were critical to the further development of each child within the classroom.

LESSON PLAN: COMMUNITY-BASED PROJECTS

Here is a sample lesson plan for a part of the previously discussed community action for UNICEF. The lesson plan format uses a five-step plan:

Goal

To increase writing skills by writing a book

Objectives

The students will

- Choose a country
- Decide on the book topic
- Discuss a story line
- Assign tasks

Materials Needed

Large paper, markers, atlas, variety of books about children in other countries

Activity

Motivation: Review letter from UNICEF and discuss reasons why this project was chosen.

Sequence:

1. The children will list names of countries that they know about and might use as background for the story.
2. Vote on the country.
3. List the topics that might be used as a basis for the story.
4. Vote on the topic.

5. Brainstorm ideas for the story. Some may want to draw pictures.
6. Vote on the general plot of book.
7. Discuss the attributes of the group, and assign tasks. Possibly they will develop a time line.

Closure: Vote on the time line for work. Find time to meet again after work has begun.

Evaluation (completed after lesson)

Self: Group discussion went well. Problem-solving strategy of drawing helped the visual learners.

Student: Nora did not volunteer, but did answer direct questions. Check during this work to be sure she is involved and interested in the project. Marcus used nonstandard English twice during the discussion. Check his future oral work.

Learnings that are focused on student interests and based on problem solving are meaningful, exciting, and interesting for young children. Practicing the skills of problem solving will provide children with a firm foundation for finding their place in the world. Actively involving children in problem solving during the early years of their life provides them with skills and knowledge that they can use to further their education and, even more important, to establish a better world.

SUMMARY

As a dynamic learning process, problem solving has many benefits for children. It offers them the opportunity to increase self-esteem, autonomy, and a feeling of competence. It focuses on the action of the child in investigating, discovering, and initiating understanding. Peer interactions and cooperative learning are powerful environments for supporting problem solving in the classroom. Learning is meaningful because teachers create a child-centered, integrated curriculum in which reciprocity and mutual respect are emphasized.

The use of problem-solving strategies has far-reaching social benefits, not only for children, but beyond the classroom as well. Galinsky (1989) describes these benefits in terms of family life. Those parents and children who develop an ability to solve problems in view of extremely difficult life experiences cope much better than others. Avoiding difficulties in life is not always possible, but learning how to stand up to problems and develop strategies for finding solutions is extremely valuable. Whether it is dealing with a difficult child, deciding how to handle aggression, or coping with issues of divorce, parents, teachers, and children will have an easier time if they know how to use strategies for solving problems. Learning how to handle difficulties is what is important.

Galinsky also discusses a study on preschool children that makes a case for connecting problem-solving ability with children's social and emotional development. Researchers demonstrate that problem solving translates into a variety of positive behaviors for children. Children were found to be better adjusted in school when they had experienced training the year before. In fact, children who were encouraged to use problem-solving skills every day in the natural life of the classroom could be distinguished from other children who did not receive such training. It is possible for overstimulated children to curb impulsivity and for withdrawn children to express themselves more forcefully when they learn to seek many alternative solutions to problems.

Supporting children's ability to use multiple solutions to problems has proved to be a useful and critical life skill. Learning to develop problem-solving skills, which dramatically enhance the quality of life, begins when teachers incorporate a problem-solving approach in the classroom with young children.

BIBLIOGRAPHY

Ames, L. B., and Ilg, F. L. *Your Four Year Old: Wild and Wonderful.* New York: Dell, 1976.

Bowers, C. "Organizing Space for Children". *Texas Child Care Quarterly 1990,* 13 (4) Spring: 3–22.

Bredekamp, S., ed. *Developmentally Appropriate Practice in Early Childhood Programs Serving Children from Birth Through Age Eight.* Expanded ed. Washington, D.C.: National Association for the Education of Young Children, 1987.

Bromley, K. *Webbing with Literature.* Boston: Allyn & Bacon, 1991.

Burns, M., and Tank, B. *A Collection of Math Lessons from Grades 1 Through 3.* New York: New Math Solutions Publications, 1988.

Copple, C.; Sigel, I.; and Saunders, R. *Educating the Young Thinker.* Hillsdale, N.J.: Lawrence Erlbaum Associates, 1984.

Derman-Sparks, L., and the A.B.C. Task Force. *Anti-bias Curriculum Tools for Empowering Young Children.* Washington, D.C.: National Association for the Education of Young Children, 1989.

DeVries, R. "What Will Happen . . .? Using a Piagetian Approach to Inspire Reasoning." In *Pre-K Today,* New York: Scholastic, 1987.

DeVries, R., and Kohlberg, L. *Programs of Early Education.* New York: Longman, 1987.

Dewey, J. *Democracy and Education.* New York: Free Press [1916], 1966.

Duckworth, E. *The Having of Wonderful Ideas and Other Essays on Teaching and Learning.* New York: Teacher's College Press, 1987.

Erikson, E. *Childhood and Society.* 2d. ed. New York: W. W. Norton, 1963.

Forman, G., and Kuschner, D. *The Child's Construction of Knowledge: Piaget for Teaching Children.* Washington, D.C.: National Association for the Education of Young Children, 1983.

Galinsky, E. "Problem Solving." *Young Children* 44 no. 4 (1989): 2–3.

Goffin, S., with Tull, C. "Problem Solving." *Young Children* 40 no. 3 (1985): 28–32.

Johnson, D. W.; Johnson, R.; Holubec, E.; and Roy, P. *Circles of Learning.* Alexandria, Va.: Association for Supervision and Curriculum Development, 1984.

Jorde-Bloom, P. *Living and Learning with Children.* Lake Forest, Ill.: New Horizons, 1989.

Kamii, C., ed. *Achievement Testing in the Early Grades: The Games Grown-Ups Play.* Washington, D.C.: National Association for the Education of Young Children, 1990.

Kamii, C., and DeVries, R. "Piaget for Early Education." In *The Preschool in Action*, edited by M.C. Day and R.K. Parker, 365–420. 2d. ed. Boston: Allyn Bacon, 1973.

———. *Group Games in Early Education.* Washington, D.C.: National Association for the Education of Young Children, 1980.

Kantrowitz, B., and Wingert, P. "How Kids Learn." *Newsweek*, April 17, 1990, 50–57.

Katz, L., and Chard, S. *Engaging Children's Minds: The Project Approach.* Norwood, N.J.: Ablex, 1989.

Krogh, S. *The Integrated Early Childhood Curriculum.* New York: McGraw-Hill, 1990.

Lay-Dopyera, M., and Dopyera, J. *Becoming a Teacher of Young Children.* New York: McGraw-Hill, 1988.

Lovitt, C., and Clarke, D. *The Mathematics Curriculum and Teaching Professional Development Package, Program Activity Bank 2.* Canberra, Australia: Curriculum Development Centre, 1988.

Mayesky, M.; Neuman, D.; and Wlodkowski, R. *Creative Activities for Young Children.* Albany, N.Y.: Delmar, 1980.

Naisbitt, J., and Aburdene, P. *Megatrends 2000.* New York: Morrow, 1990.

Ogle, D. M. "KWL: A Teaching Model That Develops Active Reading of Expository Text." *Reading Teacher* 39, no. 6 (1986) (February): 557–64.

Ramsey, P. G. *Teaching and Learning in a Diverse World.* New York: Teacher's College Press, 1987.

Rogers, D.; Sheerer Perrin, M.; and Waller, C. "Enhancing the Development of Language and Thought Through Conversations with Young Children." *Journal of Research in Childhood Education* 2; no. 1 (1987): 17–29.

Saracho, O. N., and Spodek, B. *Understanding the Multicultural Experience in Early Childhood Education.* Washington, D.C.: National Association for the Education of Young Children, 1983.

Seefeldt, C. *Social Studies for the Preschool-Primary Child.* 2d ed. Columbus, Ohio: Charles E. Merrill, 1984.

Taylor, B. *A Child Goes Forth.* Provo, Utah: Brigham Young University Press, 1980.

Teale, W., and Sulzby, G. "Emergent Literacy as a Perspective for Examining How Young Children Become Writers and Readers." In *Emergent Literacy,* edited by W. Teale and G. Sulzby. Norwood, N.J.: Ablex, 1986.

Williams, C., and Kamii, C. "How Do Children Learn by Handling Objects?" *Young Children* November 1986: 23–26.